WHAT WOULD JESUS EAT?

WHAT WOULD JESUS EAT?

DON COLBERT, M.D.

THOMAS NELSON
Since 1798

NASHVILLE   DALLAS   MEXICO CITY   RIO DE JANEIRO

This book is not intended to provide medical advice or to take the place of medical advice and treatment from your personal physician. Readers are advised to consult their own doctors or other qualified health professionals regarding the treatment of their medical problems. Neither the publisher nor the author takes any responsibility for any possible consequences from any treatment, actions, or application of medicine, supplement, herb, or preparation to any person reading or following the information in this book. If readers are taking prescription medications, they should consult with their physicians and not take themselves off of medicines to start supplementation without the proper supervision of a physician.

Published in Nashville, Tennessee, by Thomas Nelson. Thomas Nelson is a registered trademark of Thomas Nelson, Inc.

Thomas Nelson, Inc., titles may be purchased in bulk for educational, business, fund-raising, or sales promotional use. For information, please e-mail SpecialMarkets@ThomasNelson.com.

All Scripture quotations are from THE NEW KING JAMES VERSION unless otherwise designated. © 1982 by Thomas Nelson, Inc. Used by permission. All rights reserved.

Library of Congress Cataloging-in-Publication Data

Colbert, Don.
        What would Jesus Eat? : the ultimate program for eating well, feeling
    great, and living longer / by Don Colbert.
            p. cm.
        Includes bibliographical references (p.   ).
        ISBN 0-7852-6567-8 (hc)
        ISBN 0-7852-6334-9 (ie)
        ISBN 0-7852-7319-0 (sc)
            1. Nutrition—Religious aspects—Christianity. I. Title.
    BR115.N87 C65 2002
    241'.68–dc21   2002000867

Printed in the United States of America
10 11 12 13 14 EPAC 19 18 17 16 15

This book is dedicated to my father, Don Colbert Sr., for the love and discipline that he imparted to me. He was also instrumental in leading me to a personal relationship with Jesus.

CONTENTS

INTRODUCTION

WHAT WOULD JESUS EAT?

WHAT WOULD JESUS DO?

This question has been asked millions of times in recent years. We read the question or see the acronym for it—WWJD—on everything from bumper stickers to bracelets.

Most Christians I know truly want to understand what Jesus would do, and they truly want to follow His example in any given situation.

We certainly want to love and honor our heavenly Father as Jesus did.

We want to obey the Ten Commandments as He did.

We want to learn how to love other people as He did, and how to help them in both miraculous and mundane ways.

We want to follow Jesus' teachings when it comes to the use of our time, our talents, and our financial resources.

But do we want to eat as Jesus ate?

Why shouldn't we? We seek to follow Jesus in every other area of our lives. Why not in our eating habits?

Jesus cared about the health of people. Certainly His many healing miracles are testimony to that fact. He desired that people be made whole, and that included being whole in body as well as in mind and spirit.

But did Jesus actually teach anything about nutrition or how we should eat?

My contention is that He did—not necessarily by what He said, but by what He did. There are hundreds of examples throughout the Bible of practices related to healthy eating. Jesus embodied them fully in His lifestyle.

Even casual readers of the Bible know of many stories that refer to food as part of, or the main focus of, the story. Jesus taught key spiritual principles using a number of food analogies. He also participated in biblical feasts and celebratory meals. At the Last Supper, He instituted a ritual that involved food as the most sacred memorial of His death.

The medical and scientific facts confirm it. If we eat as Jesus ate, we will be healthier. He is our role model for good habits in eating, exercising, and living a healthy, balanced life.

"But," you may be saying, "times have changed since Jesus walked the earth two thousand years ago. Technology has advanced. We have many new foods today that Jesus didn't know about. Our eating patterns are vastly different."

Yes . . . and no. Times have changed and our eating patterns are different, but that isn't necessarily a good thing!

When you think of the American diet, of what do you think? Generally, we eat three large meals a day. Most people in other nations eat only two meals a day.

When you think of Southern cooking, of what do you think? Almost everything is fried. Fried chicken, fried country ham, fried potatoes, fried onions and other vegetables. Added to that are biscuits high in fat, covered with butter, and mashed potatoes smothered in rich milk gravy.

When you think of a good meal, of what do you think? Usually, in our minds, a good meal is one that includes dessert. Many Americans do not consider a meal to be proper or complete without something sweet at the end.

When you think of the American diet, that is not the way Jesus ate. Instead, the way we are eating has put us into the fast lane of health decline.

In 1901, the United States was classified as the healthiest nation in the world among one hundred nations studied. By 1920, we had dropped to second place. By 1950, we were in third place. By 1970, we were in forty-first place. And in 1981, we had dropped all the way to ninety-fifth place![1]

How does a nation go from being in forty-first place in the area of good health to being in ninety-fifth place in only eleven years? And from first place to ninety-fifth place in just one century? The answer can be summed up in two words: *fast food*.

The typical American now consumes three hamburgers and four orders of French fries every week.[2]

In 1970, Americans as a whole spent approximately $6 billion on fast food. In 2000, we spent more than $110 billion. We spend more money on fast food than we do on personal computers, computer software, new cars, and higher education combined. We also spend more on fast food than on all magazines, books, movies, newspapers, videos, and recorded music combined.[3]

The reason fast food has risen in popularity so dramatically is simple—our fast pace of life almost demands it. People feel they are too busy to prepare traditional meals, and they see fast-food meals as time-saving alternatives. In addition, many times it costs more per serving to prepare a traditional meal than to purchase a single serving at a fast-food restaurant. This is due to the fact that most of us do not routinely prepare home-cooked meals, and so we may waste much of the food we bring home from the market.

In our culture, advertisements constantly bombard us and often fuel our desire for fast food. Incentives are offered to children in the form of toys included with a meal and playgrounds just outside the restaurant. Furthermore, a fast-food restaurant is usually never more than a mile or two away. The end result is that good nutrition is sacrificed to convenience, cost, and accessibility.

Fast food is designed to appeal to these four senses: sight, smell, taste, and touch, or texture. One of the primary ways of adding both taste and texture to food is to add fat. One of the key ways of adding taste to food is to add sugar. Foods that have a glaze or a glow to them—from donuts to cake icing—are foods that have had a layer of fat added to them. In addition to having virtually no nutritional value, fast foods tend to be high in salt and low in fiber.

Eating a diet high in salt, low in fiber, very high in fat and sugar, and virtually void of nutrients is not the way Jesus ate.

THE VALUE OF A PRIMITIVE DIET

Would we really be healthier if we ate a more primitive diet—the sort of diet that Jesus ate?

Medical science says that we would.

Nearly seven decades ago, Dr. Weston A. Price reported a study that is still valid and still amazing. Dr. Price, a dentist, studied primitive people who were isolated from Western civilization, including people in Switzerland and Scotland who lived in villages and towns that were isolated from their nation's mainstream societies. Some of the cultures he studied consumed diets that included fish, seafood, and wild game; other cultures had diets that included the meat and dairy products of domesticated animals. Some cultures had diets that included fruits, grains, legumes, and vegetables; other primitive groups consumed almost no plant foods. Some primitive cultures consumed foods that were eaten raw; others consumed mostly cooked foods.

All of the cultures, however, had diets that shared certain characteristics: there were no refined, devitalized foods such as white sugar or white flour, no pasteurized or homogenized milk, no canned foods, and no hydrogenated or refined vegetable oils. All of the diets did include some animal products, and all did include salt. These isolated groups of people preserved their food using salt, fermentation, and drying methods, all of which maintained a high nutritional value of the food.

In all, Dr. Price investigated some seventeen cultures including Eskimos in Alaska, African tribes, Australian Aborigines, traditional American Indians, peoples of the South Sea Islands, those living in remote Swiss villages, and those living on remote islands off the coast of Scotland.

Dr. Price analyzed the diets of these isolated groups of people and then compared them to the American diet of his day. Keep in mind that he conducted his research in the 1930s and 1940s when the nutritional value of the American diet was actually much higher than it is now.

Here's what Dr. Price found:

· All of the so-called primitive diets contained at least four times the quantity of minerals and water-soluble vitamins as the American diet.

· All of the diets contained at least ten times the amount of fat-soluble vitamins in the American diet.

· People in these isolated cultures had virtually no tooth decay, and they had a high resistance to disease.

In some cases, Dr. Price had the opportunity to study those who had recently been introduced to processed, Westernized foods. He found that when Western civilization reached these remote areas and the diet began to include processed and sugary foods, the number of dental cavities rose rapidly. Not only was tooth decay more prevalent, but disease in general began to increase. Children born to parents who had consumed the processed food had a greater number of instances of facial and jaw deformities. A higher percentage of birth anomalies began to occur, and both acute and chronic diseases were recorded in increased numbers. The more refined the food, the faster the health of the people declined.

Dr. Price concluded that dental decay was due primarily to nutritional deficiencies, and that the same conditions that promoted tooth decay also promoted disease in general. He became a strong advocate for Americans to change their eating habits by

- choosing untampered, nutrient-dense foods.

- avoiding foods that have been processed or refined.

- choosing foods that are in their natural, fresh state.

These are the same eating habits that were the foundation of Jesus' diet!

The diet plan presented in this book is an approach to food that emphasizes the following:

1. Whole foods

2. Fresh foods

3. Pure water and foods without pesticides, fungicides, or any type of additives

4. Foods that have not been laced with sugar or infused with fat, salt, additives, or chemical preservatives

This book presents "the Jesus way of eating."

If you truly want to follow Jesus in every area of your life, you cannot ignore your eating habits. It is an area in which you can follow Him daily and reap great rewards for doing so. Following Jesus in your diet requires a commitment to change, a commitment to be all that God created you to be, and a commitment to yield your desires to God's instruction. God, in turn, will honor your heartfelt commitment by giving you more energy, better health, and a greater sense of well-being.

Are you willing to make a commitment to follow Jesus' example and eat the way He ate? If you are, then turn the page and let's begin.

CHAPTER ONE

SERIOUSLY QUESTION WHAT YOU EAT

PERHAPS THE MOST IMPORTANT STEP IN LEARNING how to follow Jesus' example and eat the way He ate can be summed up in two important questions.

Ask yourself these two key questions about everything you eat today:

1. Why do I eat this?

2. Would Jesus eat this?

If you will ask, and honestly answer, these two questions about every bite of food you put into your body, you will be forced to confront two main truths about the way you are living:

Truth #1: Most of what we eat flows from ill-founded, unwise, and mostly unconscious food choices.

Truth #2: Most of what we eat in a given day may not be what Jesus would have eaten if He were walking in our shoes.

I challenge you to take a serious look at why you eat what you eat.

THE ORIGIN OF OUR FOOD PREFERENCES

Our own memories tend to work against us when it comes to making wise food choices.

A person's food preferences are actually formed during the first four to five years of his or her life. In other words, what Mom and Dad fed us as toddlers is likely to be what we prefer the rest of our lives. We often like our food to have the color, texture, smell, and flavor of foods that we knew as young children. We may subconsciously associate these foods with fun, carefree days in which we felt secure and had few anxieties.

In adulthood, people remember the aroma or taste of the cake, ice cream, chocolate bars, pizza, hamburgers, hot dogs, and other foods they were routinely fed as children. They can be irresistibly drawn to these foods when the aroma of them is in the air. Just take a look at the foods offered at county and state fairs, and the people who are standing in long lines to purchase them!

We eat mostly out of habit. And many of our habits related to eating are bad habits.

We Have a Bad Habit of Eating Highly Processed Foods

We call them "convenience foods" for the most part. But in actuality, virtually all convenience foods are highly processed foods.

Approximately ten thousand new processed foods are introduced every year in the United States. About nine out of ten of these new food products fail—not because they are nutritionally inferior, but because they suffer a lack of successful marketing.[1] In other words, we would probably eat even more highly processed foods if we knew enough about them to give them a try!

As a physician, I have a strong conviction that America's fast-food diet and its dependence on processed foods is the primary reason for the epidemic of the widespread and serious diseases we see in our society today. These adverse health conditions include this "top fifteen" list: obesity, heart disease, cancer, diabetes, hypertension, high cholesterol, attention deficit disorder, gastroesophageal reflux disease, gallbladder disease, diverticulosis, diverticulitis, arthritis, chronic fatigue syndrome, fibromyalgia, and addictions. Almost all other degenerative diseases could be included in this list. It is difficult to find a family that has not been affected by one or more of these diseases. It is also difficult to find a family that doesn't consume a significant quantity of fast-food meals or a significant percentage of processed foods. As a physician, I do not see this as a coincidence.

Are you aware that the three most commonly consumed foods in America are white bread, coffee, and hot dogs?[2] Americans may very well be the most overfed yet undernourished people on earth. Both children and adults in our nation include large quantities of empty-calorie foods— foods that have bulk but no genuine nutritional value to the human body—in their diets. These foods range from chips to sodas, white bread to French fries, crackers to cookies, high-sugar cereals to margarine—to name only a few of the major empty-calorie food culprits.

So what's wrong with fast food or processed foods? Their consumption leads to a diet that is excessive in sugar and salt, excessive in the wrong kinds of fat, and excessive in food additives. When these foods are combined with an unhealthy percentage of meats and dairy foods—also common to the American diet—you have health problems in the making.

We in the medical world see the problem not only in the lab reports and pathology reports we read, but in the flesh every day in our clinics and private-practice offices. We see a growing number of American adults who are either significantly overweight or morbidly obese. Indeed, half of all Americans now fall into these two categories. We also see an alarming number of children who are overweight or obese—nearly one in four—and a growing number of children and adults who are developing Type II diabetes, which is directly related to dietary choices.

Are you aware that both airline companies and sports stadiums have embarked on major renovation projects to have larger seats installed simply because an increasing percentage of the public is overweight?

Statistics tell us that approximately half of all Americans alive today will die of heart disease, and approximately a third of us will develop cancer at some time in our lives.

We are exporting our problem. American fast-food chains have sprouted up across the globe. And the greater the number of fast-food chains and outlets in other nations, the greater the percentage of obesity in their populations. From 1984 to 1993 the number of fast-food restaurants in Great Britain nearly doubled, and so did the incidence of obesity.[3] In China, the number of overweight teenagers has nearly tripled in the past decade. In that same decade, Western foods were introduced and consumed in large quantities. In Japan, the youth and even many adults appear to be abandoning the traditional Japanese diet of vegetables, soy products, fish, and whole-grain rice in favor of a more Western diet. The result—the rate of obesity among Japanese children has doubled.[4]

The danger of empty calories is not simply that these foods do nothing nutritionally for the body, but that they rob the body of essential nutrients that may be stored in the body.

Many times food cravings are a sign of a nutrient deficiency. For example, simple sugars and many processed foods are deficient in B vitamins. All naturally occurring whole-grain carbohydrate foods inherently have significant amounts of B vitamins. When we consume processed foods that have had the B vitamins removed from them as part of the processing procedures, and when we consume great amounts of sugar, we find ourselves generally without adequate B vitamins. Because we need the B vitamins, if we don't get them in adequate supply through supplementation, we tend to crave even more carbohydrates in the hope that they will supply the necessary nutrients.

We Have a Bad Habit of Eating Way Too Much Sugar and Other Sweeteners

The average American consumed about 150 pounds of sugar last year. The amount of sucrose, or white table sugar, is actually in decline, but the consumption of other sweeteners, such as high-fructose corn syrup, is increasing rapidly. In addition to high-fructose corn syrup, which is present in many soft drinks, the ingredients often seen on the labels of processed and sweet foods are actually sugars: fructose, glucose, dextrose, corn syrup, sucrose, barley malt, beet sugar, rice syrup, and honey. Sugar alcohols, which have a sweet taste but are not as easily metabolized as sugar, include sorbitol, mannitol, and xylitol. Many times these sugar alcohols are associated with gas, abdominal bloating, and diarrhea.

Sweeteners, including the chemical sweeteners known as NutraSweet, saccharin, and Splenda, are added to products—most notably those labeled "sugar free."

NutraSweet, or aspartame, is by far the most popular artificial sweetener in America. It is nearly two hundred times sweeter than table sugar by volume. NutraSweet contains two amino acids: phenylalanine and aspartic acid, as well as methanol. In the body, these elements produce substances that are identical in composition to wood alcohol and formaldehyde (yes, the embalming fluid). NutraSweet has been correlated to headaches, dizziness, behavioral changes, sleeping problems, visual problems, mood swings, insomnia, ringing in the ears, confusion, brain abnormalities, and birth anomalies. It is not recommended for pregnant or nursing women, or infants younger than six months old.[5]

Saccharin is another artificial sweetener that has been available for more than a hundred years. It is three hundred to seven hundred times sweeter than sucrose. It usually has a bitter aftertaste. Large doses of saccharin have been linked to bladder cancer in experimental animals.

The newest artificial sweetener to be widely distributed is Splenda, or sucralose. Sucralose is produced by chlorinating sucrose. There is no long-term human research on Splenda; according to The Medical Letter on Drugs and Therapeutics, "its long-term safety is unknown." Sucralose is not yet approved for use in most European countries, where it is still under review, but it is being widely distributed in the United States. Research in laboratory rats, mice, and rabbits has shown that sucralose may cause numerous problems: up to 40 percent shrinkage of the thymus glands, enlarged liver and kidneys, atrophy of lymph follicles in the spleen and thymus, increased cecal weight, reduced growth rate, decreased red blood cell counts, hyperplasia of the pelvis, extension of the pregnancy period, aborted pregnancy, decreased fetal body and placenta weights, and diarrhea.[6]

Virtually all of these chemical sweeteners, especially NutraSweet, have been shown to have addictive tendencies. Many anecdotal studies have been published reporting that the more diet drinks a person consumes, the more that person craves diet drinks. One irony associated with these sweeteners is that they tend to be related to increased sugar consumption. NutraSweet especially has been shown to increase the craving for sugar.

We Eat Way Too Many Additives in Our Foods

A common statement made on processed foods is that the product has been enriched by adding vitamins or minerals. Rarely are these vitamins and minerals in a form that can be easily utilized by the human body.

What is actually added to processed foods? Sugars and other sweeteners are added to improve taste and, in some cases, to create an addiction to the food. Sweeteners are among the most common food additives and are consumed in the largest volume. The bulk of sweeteners is used in processed cakes, pies, sodas, and breakfast cereals.

Flavorings are added to improve taste or even in some cases to create taste. For example, most products that are identified as "strawberry" actually have no strawberry in them at all! More than two thousand different flavorings are available on the market today—more than fifteen hundred are synthetic, and approximately five hundred are natural.

Coloring agents are added to create greater visual appeal.

In many cases, salt and hydrogenated fats are added to improve texture and taste. This is especially true for products that are labeled "reduced sugar" or "no sugar." In the vast majority of cases, processed foods with these labels are not lower in calories at all—the sugar has simply been replaced with increased amounts of fat.

Preservatives are added to extend shelf life.

In fact, more than three thousand different additives are routinely added to our foods.

Let me assure you, Jesus did not eat processed foods, too much sugar, or food additives. What He did eat was a diet based upon biblical principles that were focused on health and wholeness for the physical body. I am 100 percent convinced that if dietary laws of the Bible were being issued by God today, there would be a "thou shalt not" attached to processed foods high in sugar, hydrogenated fat, salt, or additives.

AN EATING PLAN BASED ON LEVITICAL LAW

The foods that Jesus ate were based on Levitical law, the law that was given to the Israelites from God through Moses. The foods that Jesus ate in accordance with the law provided Him with the raw materials to produce a healthy body and a healthy mind. He lived and walked in divine health. The good news for us is this: the ancient dietary secrets associated with Jesus' way of living can bring us to greater health today!

"But," you may be saying, "I don't live under the law. I live under grace!"

Let me respond this way: God is giving you the grace today to learn about His law and to live according to it. The law that Jesus fulfilled completely in His own life and death had to do with our spiritual atonement. We no longer need to sacrifice animals or shed blood in order to experience the forgiveness of our sins. Jesus became the sacrifice for our sin on the cross. When we accept His sacrifice, we are freed from the bondage of sin in our lives, and we are empowered by God to enter into a new relationship with Him and live a new life.

Accepting Jesus as our Savior and Lord, however, does not "free" us from keeping the Ten Commandments. Rather, we are empowered to want to keep them and to actually keep them! The same is true for the other laws in the Old Testament that are not directly related to our spiritual salvation. Accepting Jesus empowers us to want to keep these laws and to actually keep them. The apostle Paul made it very clear in his letters that we are not freed from the law in order to sin further; we are freed by Christ in order to keep from sinning.

I routinely encounter Christians who know very little about what the Levitical Law says about food. They do not regard biblical dietary laws as being applicable to them, although they accept the Bible's morality laws as being applicable.

The Levitical law relating to food actually goes all the way back to the first chapter of the Bible.

GOD'S INITIAL PLAN FOR OUR BEST HEALTH

God's initial plan was for man to be a vegetarian. In the first chapter of the Bible we read, "See, I have given you every herb that yields seed which is on the face of all the earth, and every tree whose fruit yields seed; to you it shall be for food" (Gen. 1:29).

In addition, God's initial plan for every living creature was for it to be a herbivore. We also read in Genesis, "To every beast of the earth, to every bird of the air, and to everything that creeps on the earth, in which there is life, I have given every green herb for food" (Gen. 1:30).

Those who lived during this vegetarian period—from Adam to Noah—lived very long lives. Adam lived 930 years, Seth 912 years, Enos 905 years, Jared 962 years, and Methuselah 969 years, the longest recorded life span in the Bible.

After the Flood, people began to live much shorter periods of time. Abraham lived 175 years and Moses lived 120 years. Certainly the present life expectancy of about 75 years is much lower still.

There are a number of speculations about why men lived to such an old age in the vegetarian period. Some speculate that the oxygen of the earth was much greater at the time before the Flood—each breath these ancient ancestors took probably had a far greater percentage of oxygen than even the deepest breath we could take today. Some speculate that there was a moisture barrier around the earth that resulted in a higher barometric pressure. This would have been an ideal environment for plant and human growth. There is also speculation that the world before the Flood had vegetation that was extremely dense in nutrients. Those who lived from the time of Adam to the time of Noah may very well have had access to fruits and vegetables that were much richer in vitamins, minerals, and phytonutrients.

The shift after the Flood also included the introduction of meat into the human diet—a factor that may be linked to a shorter life span. When the flood waters receded and Noah and his family left the ark, Noah built an altar to the Lord and offered on it burnt offerings of clean beasts and fowl. The Lord responded by promising never to curse the earth again with a flood. He blessed Noah and his sons and said,

> Be fruitful and multiply, and fill the earth. And the fear of you and the
> dread of you shall be on every beast of the earth, on every bird of the air,

on all that move on the earth, and on all the fish of the sea. They are given into your hand. Every moving thing that lives shall be food for you. I have given you all things, even as the green herbs. But you shall not eat flesh with its life, that is, its blood. (Gen. 9:1–4)

God did not limit the meat for Noah and subsequent generations to simply "clean" meats, but indicated that every moving thing could be considered meat. Certainly there was a very practical aspect to this. Animals came off the ark and were available to Noah and his family. However, plants still needed to be cultivated, and in the case of vineyards and fruit trees, it would be years before fruit was available.

We Were Created to Be Omnivores

Man, from the time of his creation, was an omnivore, capable of living on both plant and animal foods. Our physical anatomy has been engineered, however, in such a way that we are better suited for consuming more plant products than animal products.

Human beings have twenty molars, which are teeth used for crushing and grinding plant foods. We have eight frontal incisors, which are used for biting into fruits and vegetables. Only four of our teeth, the canine teeth, are designed for eating meat. Our jaws move both vertically and horizontally to tear and crush our food—a true carnivore's jaw only moves vertically.

The human intestinal tract is about four times longer than a person is tall, which favors the ingestion of plant foods. A true carnivore's intestinal tract is much shorter and is only about two to three times the length of its body. A carnivore's stomach has as much as four times the amount of hydrochloric acid as an herbivore's stomach. Carnivores are thus able to digest meat more rapidly and eliminate waste products more quickly through a shortened gastrointestinal tract.

Nonhuman primates—such as monkeys, gorillas, and chimpanzees—are omnivores. They eat primarily fruits and vegetables, and only rarely consume small animals, eggs, and lizards. The gorilla consumes only about 1 percent of its total calories as animal foods, and the orangutan consumes about 2 percent of its food as animal products. We human beings, however, tend to consume more than 50 percent of our calories from animal foods. In this area, we need to take a lesson from the apes![7]

Our hands are similar to those of other primates and are meant primarily for picking food such as fruits, vegetables, seeds, leaves, and grains. We do not have claws for ripping flesh.

Our saliva is alkaline and contains ptyalin, which helps us digest carbohydrates. The saliva of carnivores is acidic.

Carnivores also have larger kidneys and livers than human beings in order to handle the amount of excessive uric acid and nitrogenous waste from a diet of animal foods. The liver of a carnivore secretes much greater amounts of bile in order to break down a high-fat meat diet.

Our bodies simply have not been created to handle a diet high in meat or meat fats.

We should also recognize that the meat our ancestors consumed was wild meat, which nearly always has a low-fat content. The fat content of wild game runs about 4 percent, whereas domestic beef, which has been fed primarily corn, has a fat content of 30 percent or higher. Wild game also contains more natural polyunsaturated fats and omega-3 essential fatty acids, both of which promote human health.

Why Do We Need Food Laws?

It was not until Moses came on the scene more than a thousand years after the time of Noah that God gave dietary instructions regarding clean and unclean animals for human consumption. These laws are clearly outlined in Leviticus 11 and Deuteronomy 14.

Apparently the animals of centuries prior to the time of Moses did not have diseases dangerous to man. But, by the time of the Israelites, the pollution and the disease level of the earth had reached the point at which animals of certain types had probably become carriers of bacteria, parasites, viruses, and toxins dangerous to man.

A QUICK REVIEW OF THE JEWISH DIETARY LAWS

Many people seem to think that much of the Law of Moses is devoted to dietary laws. Only two chapters and a few additional random verses—fewer than 150 verses in all—deal with this issue, and many of these verses are duplicates. Let's briefly revisit what God commanded.

CLEAN AND UNCLEAN ANIMALS

The Israelites were allowed to eat animals that had cloven or divided hooves and that chewed their cuds. We read in the opening verses of Leviticus 11:

And the LORD spoke to Moses and Aaron, saying to them, "Speak to the children of Israel, saying, 'These are the animals which you may eat among all the beasts that are on the earth: Among the beasts, whatever divides the hoof, having cloven hooves and chewing the cud—that you may eat. Nevertheless these you shall not eat among those that chew the cud or those that have cloven hooves: the camel, because it chews the cud but does not have cloven hooves, is unclean to you; the rock hyrax, because it chews the cud but does not have cloven hooves, is unclean to you; the hare, because it chews the cud but does not have cloven hooves, is unclean to you; and the swine, though it divides the hoof, having cloven hooves, yet does not chew the cud, is unclean to you. Their flesh you shall not eat, and their carcasses you shall not touch. They are unclean to you. (11:1–8)

The two main characteristics identified here are that a clean animal has cloven hooves and chews its cud. A cloven hoof is a divided or split hoof.

Animals that chew their cud are known as *ruminants*. A ruminant's stomach consists of four chambers. Food enters the rumen where digestion begins. It then passes to the reticulum, for more digestion and expulsion upward. The food returns to a chamber called the omasum, and finally to the abomasum where the cud passes into the duodenum and intestines. These four chambers of the stomach are analogous to a washing machine that has four cycles of washing and rinsing. By having these four chambers, ruminants are able to eliminate bacteria, toxins, parasites, and other vermin that might otherwise end up as part of the animal's flesh.

Animals that have cloven hooves but do not chew the cud were forbidden—these included coneys (rock badgers) and swine (pigs, hogs). Horses were not common to the Israelites in biblical times, and that is probably the main reason they were not mentioned by name. Horses are also unclean, because although they do not have split hooves, they do chew the cud. A number of studies have shown that horse meat often contains parasites, viruses, and bacteria. Disease is commonly associated with the consumption of horse meat in lands where it is consumed.

According to this Bible definition, clean animals include cattle, sheep, and goats. In Deuteronomy 14:4–5 specific animals are mentioned: "These are the animals which you may eat: the ox, the sheep, the goat, the deer, the gazelle, the roe deer, the wild goat, the mountain goat, the antelope, and the mountain sheep."

Additional laws related to animals are mentioned:

Animals that are called "creeping things" are forbidden for consumption. The Bible describes these animals as "the mole, the mouse, and the large lizard after its kind; the gecko, the monitor lizard, the sand reptile, the sand lizard, and the chameleon" (Lev. 11:29–30). Frankly, I don't know anybody who desires to eat those animals! (The same goes for the "flying insects" that "creep on all fours" and are prohibited in Leviticus 11:20.)

An animal must be slaughtered for consumption. An animal is not to be eaten if it dies a natural death or is killed in any way other than intentional slaughter. Deuteronomy 14:21 says, "You shall not eat anything that dies of itself; you may give it to the alien who is within your gates, that he may eat it, or you may sell it to a foreigner."

A young animal must not be boiled in its mother's milk. Deuteronomy 14:21 says, "You shall not boil a young goat in its mother's milk."

An animal must be drained of its blood before consumption. The stipulations regarding blood are found in Deuteronomy 12:15–27. Here are a few exemplary verses from that passage:

> You may slaughter and eat meat within all your gates, whatever your heart desires, according to the blessing of the LORD your God which He has given you; the unclean and the clean may eat of it, of the gazelle and the deer alike. Only you shall not eat the blood; you shall pour it on the earth like water. (vv. 15–16)

A similar command was given regarding domesticated animals:

> You may slaughter from your herd and from your flock which the LORD has given you . . . Only be sure that you do not eat the blood, for the blood is the life, you may not eat the life with the meat. You shall not eat it; you shall pour it on the earth like water. (vv. 21–24)

All animal fat was to be burned, not consumed. By animal fat, I am referring to the fat that a person can cut away from a piece of meat, not to the fat that has been naturally marbled into the meat itself. This tends to be the fat that lies immediately under the skin of an animal, and in the case of poultry, it includes the skin itself. Leviticus 3:16 tells us, "All the fat is the LORD's."

What can we conclude from these basic food laws about the way Jesus ate?

First, we can conclude that Jesus ate a great many fruits and vegetables. In fact, His diet was likely rich in whole grains and whole vegetables and fruits.

Second, we can conclude that Jesus ate only clean meat, poultry, and fish. We can also conclude from a rational look at the history of the time that He likely ate these clean meats in the proportion in which they existed at the time. Fish was plentiful, and Jesus likely ate fish as His primary meat source. Poultry was also plentiful, and that would likely have been the second most plentiful meat in Jesus' diet. Meat—in the form of beef, lamb, and goat meat—was least plentiful, and therefore would have been the least likely meat for Jesus to have eaten.

Third, we can conclude that Jesus ate only animals that had been slaughtered according to biblical methods, that He did not eat young animals boiled in the mother's milk, He did not eat animal blood, and He did not eat animal fat.

These are not difficult dietary principles to keep. They are, however, laws that most of us don't keep. (We'll explore this further in later chapters.)

ANSWERS TO OUR KEY QUESTIONS

Let's go back to the beginning of this chapter and attempt to answer our two important questions.

1. *Why do I eat what I eat?* Each of us must take a new look at why we choose to eat what we eat. Rather than continue our mindless, unconscious habits, we need to be intentional and rational about what we choose to put into our bodies. We need to take a cold, hard look at the bad habits into which we have fallen and choose to make a change when we find ourselves in error.

2. *Would Jesus eat this?* We need to ask this question often. Jesus certainly did not eat processed, high-sugar, high-fat, high-salt, low-fiber foods. He did eat many whole fruits and vegetables, whole-grain bread, fish, a little kosher meat, and some dairy products.

If you ask only these two questions about what you eat, but you ask and answer them honestly and rationally, you will be well on your way to following Jesus' example in your eating habits.

CHAPTER TWO

THE FOOD THAT
JESUS ATE
MOST OFTEN

WHEN I GET TO HEAVEN, ONE OF THE FIRST HUNDRED
questions I am going to ask God is this: What did manna look and taste
like? If possible, I'm even going to request a sample! Manna is one of
those mystery foods that I would love to subject to both medical and scientific analysis. But I have no doubt that manna was what the Bible says
it was: bread from heaven.

When Moses led the children of Israel out of Egypt to travel to
Canaan, the land promised to them by God, they encountered tremen-
dous hardship in the Sinai Peninsula. This is treacherous land even
today. It is an area of sand dunes, high limestone plateaus, and granite
mountains, some of which reach eight thousand feet above sea level. The
area is a desert wilderness, with very few sources of water. It is a land that
cannot support the growth of fruits, vegetables, or grains.

Food was supplied supernaturally to the people in the form of manna.
For forty years, manna was the primary staple of the Israelites.

God said to Moses, "Behold, I will rain bread from heaven for you. And the people shall go out and gather a certain quota every day" (Ex. 16:4). The exact amount to be gathered was set as an *omer*. Moses later told the people that they were to

remember that the LORD your God led you all the way these forty years in the wilderness, to humble you and test you, to know what was in your heart, whether you would keep His commandments or not. So He humbled you, allowed you to hunger, and fed you with manna which you did not know nor did your fathers know, that He might make you know that man shall not live by bread alone; but man lives by every word that proceeds from the mouth of the LORD. (Deut. 8:2–3)

Manna was an unknown food to the Israelites. In fact, manna became the name of the substance because when the Israelites first saw it, they said, "What is it?" The word for "what is it?" in Hebrew is *manna*. Manna appeared to them to be like small, round coriander seeds, as fine as frost. It was the color of bdellium—a pearlized white color. The people could cook it like grain—grind it on millstones or beat it in a mortar, and then cook it in pans or make cakes from it. It had the taste of "pastry prepared with oil" or "wafers made with honey" (Num. 11:8; Ex. 16:31).

When dew fell on the camp in the night, the manna appeared, and the ground was covered with it each morning. It was provided in sufficient quantity so that each person could gather up an omer of it, which was 2.2 liters or about three quarts minus a pint. Any manna left on the ground melted in the heat of the desert sun.

Manna had an interesting quality to it. It was to be gathered daily and not stored overnight, except on the night preceding the Sabbath. On the sixth day, the people were to gather two omers of manna; God apparently provided a double portion. On any other day, manna that was stored overnight would breed worms and stink—but not on the Sabbath. Surely that is one of the greatest food-related miracles of all time! (See Ex. 16:15–36.)

When Jesus taught His disciples to pray, "Give us this day our daily bread," He appeared to be making a direct reference to the provision of manna (Matt. 6:11). The breads of Jesus' time were coarse whole-grain breads, which were darker and heavier than the breads we have today. Since they were made with whole grain, including the bran and wheat germ, they had a much higher concentration of naturally occurring polyunsaturated oils. Just as manna would become wormy and smelly overnight, so the whole-grain bread in Jesus' day, with its high natural oil content, was likely to become rancid and moldy if it was not consumed daily. Eating a freshly baked loaf of whole-grain bread a day was and is a healthy way to live!

For forty years, manna was the staple of the Israelites' diet. It must have been highly nutritious to have sustained that many people for that length of time. It must have had precisely the correct balance of protein, carbohydrates, fats, vitamins, and minerals. God's promise to the people had been, "I will put none of the diseases on you which I have brought on the Egyptians" (Ex. 15:26). His provision for fulfilling that promise was through manna.

During their travels through that barren wilderness, how the people must have longed for the fulfillment of God's promise to them—a promise of "a land of wheat and barley, of vines and fig trees and pomegranates, a land of olive oil and honey; a land in which you will eat bread without scarcity, in which you will lack nothing" (Deut. 8:8–9).

Jesus knew what it meant to live in a wilderness such as the one through which the Israelites traveled. In Matthew 4 we read that Jesus was led by the Spirit into a wilderness area to be tempted of the devil. He remained in that wilderness—an uninhabited, desolate, lonely area—for forty days and forty nights, fasting the entire time. The Scripture tells us that afterward He was hungry. (See Matt. 4:1–2.)

During His stay in the wilderness, Jesus had three main encounters with Satan, each time Satan coming to Him with a temptation. The first temptation was this: "If You are the Son of God, command that these stones become bread." Jesus replied, "It is written, 'Man shall not live by bread alone, but by every word that proceeds from the mouth of God'" (Matt. 4:3–4).

Now, Jesus had been fasting, and He was extremely hungry. It is no surprise that Satan would come to tempt Jesus with the food that He craved the most to quench His hunger, the food that was the foremost staple of His diet: bread.

Jesus' statement to Satan was a direct quote of Deuteronomy 8:3, the verse in which Moses reminded the Israelites why God had given them manna. Satan's temptation was aimed at the most immediate physical need of Jesus, the need for food for His physical survival. But Jesus' response addressed the most basic of spiritual questions: Would He choose to live according to His natural impulses and needs, or would He live according to spiritual principles?

BREAD AND KING DAVID

The greatest king of Israel, King David, consumed bread regularly. In fact, more references are directly made to bread and whole grains in the life of King David than in the life of any other person in the Bible.

When David was just a boy, he was told by his father, Jesse, to take an ephah of parched corn and ten loaves of bread to the camp of his brothers. These food supplies were to sustain his brothers who were in the army of Saul, camped out in the Valley of Elah across from the army of the Philistines, led by a giant named Goliath. An ephah of parched corn consisted of about five gallons of dried grain.

The corn of Bible times was not like the corn, or maize, that we know in the United States today. Maize is native to North America, where it has been cultivated for more than three thousand years by the Native American Indians. Corn in the Bible, however, refers to different grains or seeds. Even in ancient England, the term *corn* referred to wheat, and in Scotland and Ireland, to oats. In the case of David taking corn to his brothers, the grain in question was likely dried kernels of wheat that could be munched upon directly.

Before David became king, he went through a decade of his life in which he was mostly on the run from King Saul, who desired to kill him. David and his men worked to support themselves by providing security for farmers who had flocks grazing in the areas near where David and his men hid out in caves and narrow gorges. Nabal was one man who had been protected by David. In 1 Samuel 25, David sent ten of his men to Nabal to request a food payment for the security services he and his men had provided. But Nabal refused.

When Nabal's wife, Abigail, heard of his refusal, she took it upon herself to take a food payment to David. Among the provisions were two hundred loaves of bread, two bottles of wine, five sheep, five measures of parched corn, a hundred clusters of raisins, and two cakes of figs. (See 1 Sam. 25:18.) God, through the services of Abigail, provided bread for David.

Later in his life, David left Jerusalem after his son Absalom mounted a coup to overthrow him. He and those loyal to him went to the area across the Jordan River from Jericho. The people who were native to that area brought David these provisions: "beds and basins, earthen vessels and wheat, barley and flour, parched grain and beans, lentils and

21

parched seeds, honey and curds, sheep and cheese of the herd . . . For they said, 'The people are hungry and weary and thirsty in the wilderness'" (2 Sam. 17:28–29).

In Psalm 37:25, David wrote, "I have not seen the righteous forsaken, nor his descendants begging bread." David knew this to be true from his personal experiences.

JESUS' RELATIONSHIP WITH BREAD

Bread played an important role in the life and teachings of Jesus. But a loaf of bread in Jesus' time was not the baker's loaf we find in our grocery stores today. Bread was baked on large, flat rocks, the dough stretched and twirled in a circular fashion to make a large, flat circle. (A similar working of dough can sometimes be seen in traditional Italian pizza restaurants.) The resulting loaf was larger than a pancake but thin, like paper. The pita bread of today is a modern, version of these loaves. One to three loaves of bread per person were eaten at each meal.[1]

Jesus referred to bread in a number of His teachings. Here are several examples:

Ask, and it will be given to you; seek, and you will find; knock, and it will be opened to you. For everyone who asks receives, and he who seeks finds, and to him who knocks it will be opened. Or what man is there among you who, if his son asks for bread, will give him a stone? Or if he asks for a fish, will he give him a serpent? If you then, being evil, know how to give good gifts to your children, how much more will your Father who is in heaven give good things to those who ask Him! (Matt. 7:7-11)

Jesus definitely regarded bread as a good gift.

I am the bread of life. Your fathers ate the manna in the wilderness, and are dead. This is the bread which comes down from heaven, that one may eat of it and not die. I am the living bread which came down from heaven. If anyone eats of this bread, he will live forever; and the bread that I shall give is My flesh, which I shall give for the life of the world. (John 6:48–51)

Jesus knew that bread was the staple of man's physical life; in like manner, only those who accept Jesus as their atoning sacrifice and feed upon the Bread of Life will enjoy eternal spiritual life.

Jesus and the Feast of Unleavened Bread
On several occasions, Jesus celebrated the Passover Feast with His disciples. This feast was marked by the consumption of lamb, bitter herbs, and unleavened bread.

Unleavened bread is simply bread made without yeast. Yeast, or leaven, causes dough to puff up. The end result is greater volume without greater weight.

The Passover Feast originated as the Israelites prepared to leave Egypt. The command of God through Moses was that the people should prepare one lamb, a male yearling without blemish, and roast it by fire for consumption in one night. One lamb, either a sheep or a goat, was to be consumed per household—small households were allowed to join together so that the entire roasted lamb was eaten, including its head and entrails. The lamb was to be eaten with unleavened bread and bitter herbs. It was to be eaten as the people were wearing sandals on their feet, a belt on their waist, and a staff in their hands; in other words, the meal was to be eaten in haste, eaten as if they were ready to move out on a moment's notice. (See Ex. 12.) Blood from the slain lamb was to be applied with hyssop branches to the doorposts and lintels of their entryways so that when the Angel of Death moved through Egypt that night, their households would be "passed over," and they would suffer no loss of their firstborn. Indeed, that is what happened. Pharaoh, grief-stricken over the death of his firstborn son, virtually banished the Israelites from the land after years of stubbornly refusing to let them go.[2]

The Israelites took batches of unleavened dough with them as they left Egypt, "having their kneading bowls bound up in their clothes on their shoulders" (Ex. 12:34). Their provision as they traveled to and through the Red Sea included unleavened bread baked from these batches of dough.

Moses also instructed the people that they were to keep a seven-day feast annually as a remembrance of the night they were delivered from Egypt. In fact, the first name for the Passover Feast was the Feast of Unleavened Bread (Ex. 12:17). The Israelites were to eat unleavened bread for seven days as part of this feast, and during those days, they were to have a holy consecration and were to do no work. Moses said that when their children asked why they kept this feast, the people were to explain, "It is the Passover sacrifice of the LORD, who passed over the houses of the children of Israel in Egypt when He struck the Egyptians and delivered our households" (Ex. 12:27).

Jesus at the Last Supper

On the night that Jesus was betrayed by Judas, He and His disciples ate their last supper together. We read in the apostle Paul's letter to the Corinthians about this night:

> For I received from the Lord that which I also delivered to you: that the
> Lord Jesus on the same night in which He was betrayed took bread; and

when He had given thanks, He broke it and said, "Take, eat; this is My body which is broken for you; do this in remembrance of Me." In the same manner He also took the cup after supper, saying, "This cup is the new covenant in My blood. This do, as often as you drink it, in remembrance of Me." (1 Cor. 11:23–25)

The meal that Jesus and His disciples were eating together was the last meal with leavened bread prior to the Passover Feast. Jesus died on the first day of Passover, fulfilling the meaning of the broken bread (His broken body), the slain lamb (His being the Lamb slain from the foundation of the world), and the bitter herbs (the bitterness associated with His death, as well as the offering of bitter vinegar while He was on the cross). This night before the Passover meal was the night in which all leaven was removed from the house. All utensils were scrubbed clean, all leavening agents were tossed out, and even the floors, walls, and fabrics of a house were washed. Likewise, the washing of the disciples' feet came after the supper was over—it was a symbol that Jesus was cleansing His disciples thoroughly from all the evil that lay ahead. Although they didn't realize it at the time, Jesus' washing of their feet was a sign that He alone would be crucified the next day—the lives of His intimate associates would be spared so they might move forward into the fullness of the ministry that God had for them.

In the Scriptures, leaven is referred to in both good and bad ways. Jesus said of the teaching of the Pharisees and Sadducees, "Take heed and beware of the leaven of the Pharisees and the Sadducees" (Matt. 16:5). On another occasion, however, Jesus said, "The kingdom of heaven is like leaven, which a woman took and hid in three measures of meal till it was all leavened" (Matt. 13:33). Jesus didn't have anything against bread with yeast! Most of the bread He consumed had leavening.

Jesus by the Sea After His Resurrection

After Jesus' resurrection, He joined His disciples by the Sea of Galilee for a breakfast of fish and bread. (See John 21:9–12).

Jesus and Raw Grain

Jesus and His disciples ate grains in their raw state, as recorded in Luke 6:1: "Now it happened on the second Sabbath after the first that He went through the grainfields. And His disciples plucked the heads of grain and ate them, rubbing them in their hands." To do this was entirely lawful— in biblical times, people were allowed to glean or pick freely the grain that remained in a field after harvest. These grains may still have been green, or they may have ripened after the harvest. Rubbing the grain in their hands removed the outer husk, but the bran and wheat germ remained.

WHEAT AND BARLEY

The two foremost grains used in the Old Testament were barley and wheat. Wheat is actually mentioned fifty-one times in the Scriptures. A wheat harvest is mentioned in Genesis 30:14, and a barley harvest is mentioned in Ruth 1:22.

Wheat was considered the staff of life and the king of grains. It became used as a measure of wealth. Barley, the cheaper and more plentiful of the two grains, was used by the poorer classes of people.

A family that had wheat bread was considered to be a fairly high-class family. In the time of Jesus, wheat was worth about three times more than barley. That apparently was also true seventy years later when John wrote in the book of Revelation: "I heard a voice in the midst of the four living creatures saying, 'A quart of wheat for a denarius, and three quarts of barley for a denarius; and do not harm the oil and the wine'" (Rev. 6:6).

Wheat's Nutritional Value

The nutritional breakdown of just one ounce of wheat bran is as follows:

Calories	60
Fiber	12 grams
Fat	1 gram
Potassium	410 milligrams
Carbohydrate	18 grams
Protein	5 grams

Wheat germ is high in B vitamins, iron, magnesium, zinc, chromium, manganese, and vitamin E. Just a quarter of a cup of wheat germ has five grams of fiber.

Wheat bran's high fiber content is one of the best-known dietary sources of insoluble fiber. It is an excellent means of protecting against and curing constipation. It helps prevent intestinal infections, hemorrhoids, and varicose veins, and helps guard against colon cancer. A healthy amount of wheat bran to consume is one to two heaping tablespoons per day.

Wheat As a Whole Grain

In addition to being used to make flour for bread, grains in Bible times were roasted, boiled, parched, or even eaten green from the stalk. Grains were ground, crushed, pounded, and dried to make soups, grain-based salads, casseroles, and even desserts.[3]

Bulgur wheat is a special preparation of the wheat grain that is found commonly in the Middle East. In bulgur wheat, the wheat kernels are washed, scrubbed, cracked, and then dried. The smaller grains can then be cooked or soaked in water—as they soak or cook, they swell. This grain is commonly used in making tabouli (also called "tabbouleh"), a salad prepared in Israel using bulgur wheat, olive oil, garlic, lemon juice, parsley, scallions, and other chopped fresh herbs.[4]

Another form of cracked wheat that is smaller than bulgur wheat is called couscous. This grain can also be used in making tabouli and other salads, but it is usually used as a main dish or in casseroles. Some desserts even use couscous. This grain is easily prepared by pouring boiling water over the cracked wheat or by lightly cooking it.

Nutritionally Rich Barley Bread

While we do not know with certainty that Jesus ate wheat bread, we do know that He ate barley bread. In the story of the feeding of the five thousand men—plus women and children—the miracle occurred because Jesus broke, blessed, and multiplied five barley loaves and two small fish brought to the event by a young boy. Barley loaves were also multiplied by Elisha; he multiplied twenty loaves of barley bread to feed a hundred men (See 2 Kings 4:42–44).

Roman gladiators were sometimes called *hordearii*, which means "barley eaters," because the grain was added to their diet to give them bursts of strength before their contests. Barley is considered to be one of three balanced starches (rice and potatoes being the other two) that are rich in complex carbohydrates and fuel the body with a steady flow of energy.

In some areas of the Middle East, barley has been called the "medicine for the heart." It contains fiber that can lower the risk of heart disease by reducing artery-clogging LDL (bad) cholesterol. This same high fiber content keeps a person regular, relieving constipation and warding off a variety of digestive problems. It may also help block the development of cancer.

In a study conducted at Montana State University, a group of men ate a high-barley diet, including cereal, bread, cake, and muffins made from barley flour. After consuming three servings a day of this food for six weeks, the cholesterol levels of these men were an average of 15 percent lower. Those with the highest cholesterol levels at the start of the study showed the most significant improvement. Another group of men who ate the same products made with wheat or bran flour did not have a drop in their cholesterol counts.

Look for the term *unpearled* on a box of barley grain or flour. This means that the barley is unprocessed and high in fiber. It is available at most health food stores. In contrast, barley that is labeled "Scotch" or "pearled" has been processed and is not nearly as effective.

Barley is available on the market today, but you do have to look for it. Barley bread is virtually nonexistent—you'd have to make it yourself from the grain you could find. The vast majority of barley grown today is used to feed livestock or to manufacture whiskey and beer. Barley grain is rarely eaten by itself; however, it is sometimes used as an ingredient in soups.

Other Biblical Grains

Worldwide, more than eight thousand different species of plants supply grains. Only a very small number of these grains are consumed routinely by Americans. The most commonly consumed grains worldwide are wheat, rice, corn, and oats. Rice, corn, and oats were not consumed in Israel during the time of Jesus.

Other grains mentioned in the Bible besides wheat and barley are millet and rye. Millet is mentioned only once in the Scriptures (Ezek. 4:9). As a grain, however, millet is superior to wheat, corn, and rice in protein content; its average protein content is between 10 and 12 percent. It is also high in minerals and is easily digested. Millet is a hardy plant and can grow in rich or poor soil. It requires little moisture in order to grow. Since wheat allergy is one of the most common food allergies in America today, millet is a good alternative. Millet has no gluten, which is the primary cause of wheat food allergies. Many health food stores carry millet bread. Sadly, the majority of millet grain that is produced is used as bird or chicken feed. Interesting, isn't it, that we feed our birds better grain than many of us eat ourselves?[5]

Rye is another grain mentioned in the Bible. Rye is a gluten grain, but its gluten content is much lower than that of wheat. It is approximately 20 percent protein and is high in fiber. Rye contains high amounts of the minerals magnesium, iron, and potassium. It also contains B vitamins and other minerals. Most rye breads available commercially are made with refined rye flour, and this flour has usually been mixed with processed wheat flour. Pure rye bread is difficult to find. It is nearly black in color and is very nourishing and flavorful.

WHOLE GRAINS FOR MAXIMUM HEALTH BENEFIT

When it comes to the nutritional value of grains, a very simple choice is involved: whole or refined. Rather than choose whole-grain breads, we tend to choose the refined white bread. Instead of whole-grain cereals, we tend to feed our children boxes of commercial breakfast cereals that usually have more than 50 percent of their calories in sugar and very little to no fiber. As far as I am concerned, these cereals should not even be called cereals. They should be labeled "cookies" or "candies" rather than "cereals."

Unfortunately, one saying among nutritionists is this: "The whiter the bread, the sooner you're dead." But most of us habitually choose white bread because that's what we were fed as children. Most of us don't have a clue as to how wheat is processed in order to make bread white.

THE PROCESSING OF WHEAT FOR "WHITENESS"

The processing of whole grains of wheat to white flour takes approximately twenty steps.[6] The wheat kernel is composed of an outer layer called the *bran*. The bran is rich in B vitamins, minerals, and fiber. The next layer is the wheat germ, which is the sprouting portion of the kernel. The wheat germ is a rich source of vitamins B and E. The next layer is the endosperm, which is the starch or food supply for the sprouting seed. The endosperm is approximately 80 to 85 percent of the grain. The germ is about 3 percent, and the bran about 15 percent.

Refined white flour is pure endosperm or starch. Both the bran and the germ have been removed, along with approximately 80 percent of the wheat's nutrients. The endosperm has far lower B vitamin and mineral content than the germ and bran, and also significantly less fiber.

Not only have 80 percent of the nutrients been removed, but the milling process involves such high temperatures that the remaining grain is damaged by oxidation. Flour at the end of the refining process actually has a grayish appearance from the oxidation. That color, of course, would be offensive to most consumers. So a chemical agent such as chlorine dioxide, acetone peroxide, or benzoyl peroxide is used to bleach the flour to make it white. This bleaching process destroys even more of the few vitamins that remain. In addition, the bleaches can react with fatty acids to produce peroxides that are toxic and that can cause free-radical reactions. (Just compare these bleach products to the labels on chemical bleaches in your home such as Clorox!) In all, the milling and bleaching processes used today remove some twenty-two important nutrients from our bread, including fiber, vitamins, and minerals.

The white flour, however, looks cleaner and purer than dirty brown whole wheat flour. And as a consequence, it is more appealing to the American public.

What about "enriched" bread? To these breads, bakeries usually replace about four nutrients to the flour they use—thiamin, niacin, riboflavin, and iron. However, the vitamins they use are usually "coal tar derived" vitamins. Unfortunately, the end result is extremely little actual vitamin enrichment.

Low-fiber bread that has been laced with a great deal of sugar and hydrogenated fat becomes pastelike in the intestines. This, in turn, leads to constipation, which in turn may lead to gastrointestinal disease such as irritable bowel syndrome, diverticulosis, diverticulitis, and hemorrhoids.

"But," you may be saying, "I only have a couple of slices of white bread a day." Oh, really? Are you also counting the buns for your hamburgers and hot dogs? Are you including crackers, bagels, pretzels, and many pasta and cereal products, which are also made of white flour? Remember, the most commonly eaten foods in America are white bread, coffee, and hot dogs.

The Link to Food Allergies

Gluten is the main protein found in grains. Wheat has a higher gluten content than any other grain. Oats, rye, and barley also have gluten, but it is present in lower amounts. Nongluten grains include rice, millet, buckwheat, amaranth, and quinoa. A grain with low gluten content is spelt.

Celiac disease is an intestinal disorder characterized by malabsorption and diarrhea that result from the body's inability to utilize gluten.

Allergies to grains may be the result of excessive consumption of processed foods.

Choose Whole-Grain Products!

The conclusion we can draw is this: Choose whole-grain products! Besides bread, you should be able to find whole-grain pasta, whole-grain muffins and bagels, and whole-grain pretzels. If the label on these products does not read "whole wheat" or "whole grain," you should assume that the product is made completely or partially with refined flour.

DRINKING YOUR GRAINS

Convenient and health-promoting products made available by our technology today are beverages that yield the nutritional benefit of whole grains without actually having to eat the grains. Rather, we can drink the nutritional benefits from whole grain.

Wheat grass and barley grass products are both available. At times, the juice itself can be purchased. More commonly, these products are found in powder form that can be mixed with water, juice, or another beverage. Both are rich in chlorophyll, which is the green blood of the plant. Chlorophyll is very similar to the "heme" component that is part of the hemoglobin in our blood, the part of the blood that carries oxygen. Heme in blood is bound by iron whereas chlorophyll in plants is bound by magnesium.

Extracts of wheat and barley are rich in flavonoids, which are phytonutrients. Flavonoids have been shown to have antiviral, antitumor, and anti-inflammatory properties. Chlorophyllin is quite abundant in both wheat and barley grasses. It has been shown to inhibit a number of carcinogens including those found in cigarette smoke and in charred meats.[7]

Wheat grass and barley grass powders are often packaged with chlorella, spirulina, and blue-green algae in products that are called "green foods" or "superfoods."

WHAT WOULD JESUS EAT?

Jesus ate whole grains directly and in the form of whole-grain bread. We can follow His example by choosing to eat whole-grain breads and pastas, and to eat whole grains in cooked and salad dishes.

CHAPTER THREE

A STAPLE IN
JESUS' DIET

A FEW YEARS AGO THERE WAS A POPULAR COOKBOOK that presented a hundred ways to fix hamburger. It was a best-seller. The popular book, however, in Jesus' day would likely have been *101 Ways to Fix Fish!*

Fishing was a major industry along the Jordan River and the Sea of Galilee throughout Bible times. When the Israelites were wandering in their exodus from Egypt, they also fished in the Red Sea for a time. The Hebrews were highly skilled fishermen, and several of Jesus' chosen disciples were fishermen by trade. A number of Jesus' teachings and miracles related to fishing.

We certainly know that Jesus ate clean, fresh, unpolluted fish almost every day of His life. In fact, I believe that fish and bread were two of the main foods in His diet. Why do I make this claim? Because fish was the most common meat eaten during the days of Jesus.

In the time of Jesus, the Sea of Galilee, the Mediterranean Sea, and the Jordan River were major sources of fish, and the Jewish people ate a wide variety of them. Fish were so plentiful in the markets of Jerusalem that one gate into the old city of Jerusalem was named the "Fish Gate."

The average person in Jerusalem at the time of Jesus could afford other types of meat only for special celebrations, but fish was inexpensive and, therefore, a regular part of the average person's diet. Those who lived in the Galilee area likely ate fish every day.

Jesus frequently referred to fish in His teachings. He listed fish among the "good gifts" mentioned in Luke 11:

Ask, and it will be given to you; seek, and you will find; knock, and it will be opened to you . . . If a son . . . asks for a fish, will he give him a serpent instead of a fish? . . . If you then, being evil, know how to give good gifts to your children, how much more will your heavenly Father give the Holy Spirit to those who ask Him! (Luke 11:9, 11, 13)

On several occasions, Jesus' miracles involved fish.

Twice Jesus fed multitudes of people with just a few fish. He took five loaves and two fish, blessed them, broke them, and gave them to His disciples to feed five thousand men, besides the women and children in the crowd (See Matt. 14:16–21). Later, Jesus took seven loaves and "a few little fish" and gave thanks for them, broke them, and gave them to His disciples to feed four thousand men, besides the women and children (See Matt. 15:32–37). The "little fish" may have been sardines, a small fish of the herring family. In both miracles, there were portions left over!

Some historians have estimated that as many as five hundred small fishing boats worked the Sea of Galilee in the days of Jesus. At times, their catches of fish were great.

Two great catches of fish are associated with Jesus and His disciples. In one case, Jesus borrowed a fishing boat as a teaching platform, and after He had finished with it, He advised Peter and his fishing partners to launch out into the deeper waters for a catch. Peter, a skilled and successful commercial fisherman, knew that fish avoided the nets during the bright sunlight of midday, but nevertheless, because Jesus had commanded him, he launched out into the deeper waters and cast his nets. The result was an overwhelming catch of fish, so great in fact that Peter was in awe. Jesus then said, "Come after Me, and I will make you become fishers of men" (Mark 1:17). The men immediately left their nets and followed Him.

On one occasion, Jesus sent Peter fishing with the command, "Go to the sea, cast in a hook, and take the fish that comes up first. And when you have opened its mouth, you will find a piece of money" (Matt. 17:27). Peter was further told to take that money to pay the temple taxes that the religious tax collectors claimed were owed by Jesus and His disciples (See Matt. 17:24).

Truly, fishing with Jesus had its rewards!

After the Resurrection, Jesus appeared on the shore of the Sea of Tiberius one morning. Peter and several other disciples had been fishing all night but had caught nothing. Jesus called to them from the shore and told them to cast their nets on the right side of the boat. The result was a catch so large that they were not able to bring it up into the boat. That same morning, the disciples came to shore to find that Jesus had already made a fire and cooked a breakfast of fish and bread for them.

CLEAN AND UNCLEAN FISH

The Law of Moses gave specific commands related to fish that were acceptable for human consumption:

These you may eat of all that are in the water: whatever in the water has fins and scales, whether in the seas or in the rivers—that you may eat. But all in the seas or in the rivers that do not have fins and scales, all that move in the water or any living thing which is in the water, they are an abomination to you. They shall be an abomination to you; you shall not eat their flesh, but you shall regard their carcasses as an abomination. Whatever in the water does not have fins or scales—that shall be an abomination to you. (Lev. 11:9–12)

Ritual slaughter applied only to meat and fowl, but not to fish. The defined species is what made a fish clean.

Scales can be scraped from the skin of a fish without tearing the skin from the flesh. Bony tubercles are not considered scales. Fish that have types of scales that are unclean include swordfish, sturgeon, sharks, lumpfish, and European flatfish. Fish without any scales include catfish, sculpins, and monkfish.

What About Seafood?

All crustacean and mollusk shellfish have no scales and are therefore unclean.[1] Mollusks include clams, mussels, oysters, and scallops. Crustaceans include crabs, lobsters, shrimp, prawns, and crayfish.

Raw shellfish is a major source of food poisoning in our nation, and diseases commonly carried by shellfish include salmonella and the Hepatitis A virus. Shellfish have a unique ability to purify waters of pathogenic bacteria such as cholera; many of these toxins are associated with raw sewage. Clams and oysters can filter between twenty and fifty gallons of seawater a day. The toxins, however, remain in the flesh of the shellfish.

Eating contaminated shellfish can result in paralytic shellfish poisoning. The symptoms usually begin with numbness in the lips and tongue, which eventually spreads to the arms and legs—usually with accompanying respiratory problems. Shellfish can also concentrate "red tide," leading to blood poisoning and death in high-risk patients. The red tide produces neurotoxins that are not destroyed by cooking.[2]

Unfortunately, due to consumer demands for shellfish, the fishing industry is harvesting these creatures closer to shorelines, where the pollution is much higher. Consequently, instances of shellfish poisoning are on the rise.

I personally regard shellfish as the "cockroaches of the sea"—they are miniature waste collectors for viruses, bacteria, parasites, and toxic waste products. We are not only told in Scripture to avoid them, but also that they are an "abomination" to human beings (Lev. 11:12).

Catfish Are Unclean

Catfish caught in rivers and streams are perhaps the most contaminated of all bottom-feeding fish because they are the first to ingest the industrial pollutants that sink to the bottoms of streams and rivers. Catfish now ranks fifth in consumption in the U.S. among fish, and much of what is now eaten is raised in freshwater tanks. Nevertheless, these fish are among the fish created to be cleansers of the waters. Just because a fish is raised in a tank does not mean that it is raised in pollutant-free water. Many fish are farmed near industrialized areas of the nation, and the waters in which they are grown are drawn from contaminated sources.

Like shrimp, lobsters, and all other shellfish, catfish were initially created by God to act as cleansing agents for natural water sources. These creatures have a great ability to absorb pollutants but not become sick by them. They can and do, however, pass on those pollutants to human beings who eat their flesh.

THE NUTRITIONAL BENEFITS OF FISH

On a positive note, clean fish with fins and scales are extremely beneficial for human consumption. A major multiple-risk-factor intervention trial study that involved more than thirteen thousand men in the United States revealed that the risk of dying from a heart attack was approximately 40 percent less for those who ate the most fish.

Most fish have high-quality protein and are a good source of essential nutrients such as zinc, copper, magnesium, B vitamins, and iodine, as well as other minerals.

Fish consumption has many beneficial properties. It has been shown to

- thin the blood

- protect arteries from damage

- inhibit formation of blood clots

- lower LDL (bad) cholesterol

- lower blood pressure

- reduce triglycerides

- reduce the risk of strokes and heart attack

- reduce the risk of lupus

- fight inflammation

- ease symptoms of rheumatoid arthritis

- help regulate the immune system

- relieve migraine headaches

- soothe bronchial asthma

- combat early kidney disease

- inhibit growth of cancerous tumors in animals

FISH PROVIDES ESSENTIAL FATS

Many people believe that all fat is bad for a person. This is not so. Our bodies need certain kinds of fat—especially fats called "essential fatty acids." These are called "essential" because our bodies cannot manufacture these fats directly. We need to acquire them from food sources. However, what we do not need are foods high in saturated fat.

Fish is low in saturated fat. The fat content of fish varies widely, however. Fish are nutritionally divided into three groups. "Lower-fat fish" have fewer than 5 grams of fat in a 3.5-ounce serving. "Fatty fish" have 5 to 10 grams of fat in the same size serving, and "high-fat fish" have more than 10 grams of fat for every 3.5 ounces.

Lower-fat fish include cod, flounder, haddock, halibut, perch, pollack, red snapper, sea bass, rainbow trout, and yellow fin tuna.

Fatty fish include freshwater bass, bluefish, mullet, orange roughy, and bluefin tuna.

High-fat fish include herring, mackerel, pompano, salmon, and sardines. These fish are very high in the essential omega-3 fatty acids.

A number of studies on the beneficial effects of fish oils began appearing in the mid-1980s in the prestigious *New England Journal of Medicine*. Diets high in fish oil were associated with a lower death rate from coronary heart disease.

In one such study, Eskimos in Greenland were discovered to have a heart attack rate of only 10 percent of that in the U.S. adult. Dr. J. Dyerberg, who conducted this study in the late 1970s, found that although the Eskimos he studied ate a diet rich in the oils of cold-water fatty fish and seals, they had low levels of LDL (bad) cholesterol and high levels of HDL (good) cholesterol.[3]

Fish oil contains two very important fatty acids that people are generally able to produce on their own. However, some people lose their ability to produce these because of disease or other reasons. The richest sources of these fatty acids are in fatty cold-water fish such as mackerel, sardines, salmon, herring, and pompano. The omega-3 fats make up approximately 15 to 30 percent of the oils in these fish. Omega-3 fatty acids are also found in lower-fat fish, only in smaller concentrations.

Omega-3 fatty acids have many health benefits. They help lower cholesterol and triglyceride levels. They improve blood sugar control and also improve neurotransmitter communication necessary for good brain function, including increased memory function. Specifically, fish oils make brain cell membranes more flexible, creating better communication between synapses and thus improving brain function. There is an old saying that what's good for the heart is good for the brain, and fish has been commonly called "brain food" for centuries.

Fish oils help prevent atherosclerosis, thereby helping to prevent coronary artery disease and heart attacks. They help lower triglycerides up to 65 percent. And fish oil can help lower blood pressure.

Fish oils help decrease inflammation from rheumatoid arthritis and lupus. They actually act like an anti-inflammatory medication. Fish oils decrease inflammatory substances significantly within a period of just a month. Leukotriene B$_4$ is an inflammatory substance that is one of the most powerful mediators of pain and inflammation in the body. One can decrease leukotriene B$_4$ levels with powerful medications such as prednisone, but the downside is that these medications are associated with dangerous side effects. Or a person can decrease leukotriene levels with fish oil. I'll choose the fish oil any day!

Fish oil has been shown to be beneficial in providing relief to migraine sufferers and to patients with psoriasis, asthma, glaucoma, diabetes, and many other degenerative conditions.

Fish oil may also be important in preventing certain cancers. Fish oil promotes good eicosanoids, which are immune enhancers—they decrease inflammation and the proliferation of cancer cells. Some animal studies have demonstrated that fish oil was able to block the growth and metastases of tumors.[4]

FISH OIL IS AVAILABLE IN SUPPLEMENT FORM

Jesus certainly obtained His daily dose of fish oil from the wide variety of fish He had in His diet. We have the option of obtaining the benefits of fish oil from fish, or from fish oil supplementation. Fish oil is readily available as capsules or in liquid forms of cod liver oil.

I believe that the healthiest option is to take fish oil capsules and eat fatty fish a few times a week. Taking two to four fish oil capsules a day is equal in fatty acids to eating fish high in omega-3 (salmon, mackerel, herring, sardines) two to three times a week. A single fish oil capsule typically contains about 180 mg of EPA and 120 mg DHA. If you have any of the diseases that are confronted by omega-3 oils, I recommend you take more capsules.

In choosing fish oil capsules, always choose capsules that are lighter in color and that contain vitamin E to help prevent rancidity. I personally chew my fish oil capsules to make sure they are fresh. If a fish oil capsule has a strong fish odor, it likely is rancid and should not be consumed. I always recommend that you store bottles of fish oil capsules in the refrigerator after opening them.

GUIDELINES FOR PURCHASING AND PREPARING FRESH FISH

The foremost guideline for purchasing fresh fish is making certain the fish is from pure waters.

In Ezekiel, the prophet declares a day when even the waters of the Dead Sea will have fish. It is interesting to me that Ezekiel's prophecy is related to an abundant source of pure water that was so deep it formed a "river that could not be crossed." The prophecy declares:

And it shall be that every living thing that moves, wherever the rivers go, will live. There will be a very great multitude of fish, because these waters go there; for they will be healed, and everything will live wherever the river goes. It shall be that fishermen will stand by it from En Gedi to En Eglaim; they will be places for spreading their nets. Their fish will be of the same kinds as the fish of the Great Sea, exceedingly many. (Ezek. 47:9–10)

Fishermen have known for centuries that the quality and quantity of fish they catch are directly related to the purity of the waters in which the fish spawn and live out their lives.

In purchasing fish, one of the most important things to know is where the fish has been harvested. Farm-raised or pen-raised salmon have a higher risk of being contaminated with industrial pollutants if they are grown in waters near industrialized areas. Fish from the Great Lakes as well as freshwater fish may have been grown in polluted waters or near industrialized areas of the nation, and other fish such as swordfish, tuna, and pike are more likely to contain fat-soluble pollutants such as pesticides, PCBs, and mercury.

Unfortunately, even the high-fat fish such as pompano, mackerel, salmon, and herring—if caught in polluted waters such as those common in the Northeast—can be home to fat-soluble pollutants such as pesticides, PCBs, and mercury. But the high-fat content in these fish actually causes these fish to accumulate more toxins. Lower-fat fish such as sole and flounder usually have less pollutants, as do fish harvested from clean areas in the northern Pacific. Salmon that is harvested off the coast of Alaska is much less likely to be polluted by industrial waste and PCBs than salmon from the northern Atlantic.

The waters off Mexico, Argentina, and Chile are extremely pure, as are the seas surrounding New Zealand and Iceland.

You should also know that fish raised on "fish farms" often have lower levels of omega-3 fatty acids. Cold-water salmon feed on algae, plankton, krill, and other foods that are high in omega-3 fatty acids. Sometimes fish farms feed these high-omega-3 foods to their fish; others do not.

Do Not Eat Raw Fish

Raw fish should be avoided. Raw fish often contains tapeworms and other parasites, and salting or smoking the fish may not kill all of them. It is important to cook fish adequately to destroy any parasites that may be in the flesh of the fish.

Look at Their Eyes

When purchasing fish at the supermarket, choose whole fish—unskinned—whenever possible. Look first at the eyes of the fish. They should be shiny, bright, and bulging—the eyes should be firm and clear. Then look at the scales—they should be shiny. Touch the fish. If you make a dent in the flesh of the fish when you touch it, don't buy it—the flesh should spring back to the touch. The gills of the fish should be firm and pink. And finally, smell the fish. If it smells "fishy," don't buy it. Fresh fish has almost no odor.[5] (You can ask the butcher to remove the fish's head and to debone and skin the fish while you do your other market shopping.)

Fish should be refrigerated immediately after purchase, and frozen fish should be stored no longer than a month.

Do not fry or deep-fry fish. Frying cancels out the beneficial effects of the omega-3 fatty acids. You may grill fish on a non-charcoal grill, bake it, broil it, or poach it.

Try different types of fish. There is great variety in taste among fish, something that a person realizes only if he is eating grilled, poached, baked, or broiled fish, because frying masks the taste of fish.

WHAT WOULD JESUS EAT?

Jesus ate a wide variety of fresh, clean-species fish, probably on a daily basis. He benefited from the essential fatty acids they provided. He most likely ate fish that was grilled, baked, broiled, and poached.

We can follow His example by adding more fish to our diet and by taking fish oil supplements. We must make sure that our fish comes from unpolluted waters, that it is fresh, and that we have stored and cooked it in a way that maintains maximum nutritional benefit.

CHAPTER FOUR

THE MEATS THAT
JESUS ATE

MOST OF US OVER THE AGE OF THIRTY ARE PROBABLY
familiar with the phrase made popular years ago from a TV commercial
for a fast-food restaurant: "Where's the beef?"

In light of our discussion about "the Jesus way of eating," the answer
to that question is that beef in Jesus' day was scarce and of a different type
from that found in today's fast-food hamburgers. Red meat simply was not
abundant in the Jewish diet.

Red meat was nearly always a specialty food reserved for feasts, weddings, holidays, banquets, and parties. Lambs were slaughtered annually
for the keeping of the Passover Feast.

In the story of the prodigal son, the father was so elated at his son's
return that he told his servants to "bring the fatted calf here and kill it,
and let us eat and be merry" (Luke 15:23).

Wealthy families routinely fed specific animals in anticipation of
upcoming feast days and days of sacrifice. Such animals were also kept in
the event that an "angel unaware" might show up and require a meal.

This custom came from the Jewish understanding of an event that occurred in the life of Abraham.

One day as Abraham was sitting in his tent during the heat of the day, he looked up and saw three men coming his way. He went to meet them and invited them to his tent.

Abraham ordered that their feet be washed. He gave them morsels of bread, and then told Sarah to make flour cakes for them. For his part, Abraham "ran to the herd, took a tender and good calf, gave it to a young man, and he hastened to prepare it" (Gen. 18:7). He then took butter and milk and the calf that had been prepared and set a meal before the visitors.

It was these visitors who told Abraham that he would bear a son by Sarah in the coming year. That son, Isaac, was born just as they had fore-told, even though both Abraham and Sarah were long past normal child-bearing age.

In the following generations, the Hebrew people felt it wise to always have a fatted calf on hand should a divine visitor show up at their door!

DID JESUS EAT RED MEAT?

It is very likely that Jesus ate beef since we know that many people cele-brated His presence in their homes, and we also know from Scripture that He attended weddings, where beef was often included as a feast food. Beef consumption, however, would not have been a daily or weekly prac-tice for Jesus.

For the most part, animals were not kept for their meat. Sheep and goats were valued as a source of fiber, from their wool or hair, and a source of milk. Cattle were prized for their ability to be beasts of burden. When red meat was eaten, the meat was more likely to be from a lamb or goat than from a cow or ox.

What we do know with certainty about the meat that Jesus ate is this:

1. Jesus did not eat pork or any other unclean meat.

2. Jesus did not eat meat fat.

3. Jesus did not eat the blood of slaughtered animals.

4. Jesus ate meat sparingly.

Let's take a closer look at each of these statements.

THE PROBLEM WITH PORK

Many people declare today that pork is a safe meat to eat in modern times. I disagree. Pigs eat enormous amounts of food, and this dilutes the hydrochloric acid in a pig's stomach. This in turn allows toxins, viruses, parasites, and bacteria to be absorbed into the animal's flesh. Besides being gluttons, swine are also extremely filthy animals. They will eat garbage, feces, and even decaying flesh. All that is eaten usually becomes part of the pig's own flesh. Pigs readily harbor parasites including *Trichinella*, the pork tapeworm, and toxoplasmosis.

If left alone with large quantities of food, a hog will literally eat itself to death. It has no stop button when it comes to eating. Swine are analogous to gluttons—in other words, the swine is to the animal world what the glutton is to humanity. Swine are one of the creatures that God apparently intended to be cleansers of the toxins of the earth. What they consume is to a great extent what we should not consume!

Cooking pork at temperatures of 160 degrees Fahrenheit or greater will kill the parasites, but it should be noted that the center portion of pork steaks or pork chops must be heated to this temperature or parasites will not be killed. Often this does not occur.

Trichinosis is one disease that can be contracted from undercooked pork. The main symptoms of trichinosis are muscle aches and pains, swelling of infected muscles, headaches, fever, and on occasion, gastrointestinal upset.

In Mark 5, we find the story of a demon-possessed man who lived in the country of the Gadarenes, a Roman-dominated area. When Jesus encountered this man, He asked the demons to tell Him their names, and the demons spoke through the man, saying, "Legion, for we are many."

A large herd of swine was feeding near the mountains, and the demons begged Jesus, saying, "Send us to the swine, that we may enter them" (Mark 5:12). Jesus gave them permission, and the demons entered the swine. The herd immediately ran off a steep cliff into the sea, and all of the pigs drowned.

Had the swine been clean animals, Jesus would never have allowed the demons to enter them. By sending the demons into the swine, He was simply making unclean meat even more unclean!

Also, in this Roman area, where feasts to the Roman gods were an everyday occurrence, cattle were routinely sacrificed to the "god above," and swine were sacrificed to the "god below." Jesus knew that the swine were destined to be sacrificed to the devil, and He simply sped the demons on their way back to hell.

Aside from the diseases routinely carried by swine, pork is also a very fatty meat. The toxins in pork are held especially in the fat, which is not isolated from the meat as can be the case in lean beef, but rather, it is dispersed throughout the meat. Pork products—such as bologna, bacon, and lunch meats—are often very high in fat content. This reason alone is sufficient cause to avoid eating pork!

I strongly recommend that you avoid highly processed meats, such as hot dogs, bologna, sausages, cold cuts, ham, bacon, and most packaged luncheon meats.

Hot dogs—wieners—are usually made of the waste products of meat, and many even have animal hair as part of that waste. They are highly processed, very high in fat, and usually have nitrites and nitrates added to them as part of the curing process. In the body, these nitrites and nitrates are converted to nitrosamines in the digestive tract—and nitrosamines are associated with an increased risk of cancer.

THE PROBLEM OF MEAT FAT

As noted briefly in a previous chapter, one of the strict commands concerning fat is found in Leviticus 3:16–17:

All the fat is the LORD's. This shall be a perpetual statute throughout your generations in all your dwellings: you shall eat neither fat nor blood.

Later in the book of Leviticus we find this regulation:

Speak to the children of Israel, saying: "You shall not eat any fat, of ox or sheep or goat. And the fat of a beast that dies naturally, and the fat of what is torn by wild animals, may be used in any other way; but you shall by no means eat it. For whoever eats the fat of the beast of which men offer an offering made by fire to the LORD, the person who eats it shall be cut off from his people." (7:23–25)

The Lord clearly forbade consumption of all types of fat. He was referring not to plants here, or to the fats found in fish, but to the fat from the animals declared clean for sacrifice to the Lord. What is referenced is what we call today "midriff fat," or the fat surrounding the kidneys and intestines. This fat was burned as part of the sacrifices offered in the tabernacle and the temple. The regulation does not refer to the marbled fat in clean meats, such as beef.

All animal fat is saturated fat—it has been closely linked to elevated cholesterol as well as heart disease. Americans typically eat three hamburgers a week, in addition to other forms of red meat. The meat we eat is high in saturated fat, which leads to high cholesterol, high triglycerides, and eventually cardiovascular disease.

We have absolutely no mention of Jesus ever sitting down to a juicy steak dinner, or grilling a greasy hamburger to put between two pieces of pita bread. But we do read about Jesus sitting down to meals of fish and bread. We would be wise to follow that example.

I recommend that a person eat as little animal or dairy fat as possible. When eating meat, trim any visible fat from the meat before cooking it. The same goes for poultry fat and skin.

The Value of Free-Range Meats

We need to recognize that the cattle of today are not like the cattle in Bible times. Virtually all clean animals killed for consumption in Bible times were animals that grazed on grass in open fields. Today's livestock tend to live much of their lives in large feed lots where they are closely crowded together and are fed large amounts of grain. A typical steer consumes more than three thousand pounds of grain to gain about four hundred pounds. Beef cattle are usually slaughtered at about three years of age, and veal calves at six months of age. The lives of those destined for slaughter are very simple: stand and eat day after day after day. Many animals have anabolic steroids planted in their ears to help them gain weight. Some are given a bovine growth hormone to make them larger. Antibiotics are usually included in the cattle feed so that the animals will not become infected since the lots are so crowded—any bacterial disease could sweep quickly through a feed lot.

In 1991, the Centers for Disease Control (CDC) released a startling statistic—approximately half of the fifteen million pounds of antibiotics produced annually in America are used to treat livestock and poultry.

If you choose to eat red meat, choose very lean cuts of free-range meat. Limit your consumption of red meat to only once a week, or perhaps even once a month, and consume a portion four ounces or less.

Free-range cattle have lower fat content in their meat since they exercise by walking and feeding on the open range. In other words, they are not cooped up in small pens or in overcrowded feed lots. Free-range beef does not have the overabundance of pesticides, antibiotics, or hormones that are usually fed to feed-lot animals.

Many larger chain grocery stores now offer free-range meats. You'll pay higher prices, but your health is worth it.

DISEASES ASSOCIATED WITH RED MEAT

In making our dietary choices, we should also be aware of the diseases that are associated with red meat. According to the Centers for Disease Control (CDC), food-borne pathogens cause approximately seventy-six million illnesses and approximately five thousand deaths each year in the United States! Unfortunately, the cause of many of these illnesses is due to contamination of meat by bacteria that comes from the animals' own intestinal tracts. Fecal contamination of red meat and poultry is all too common.

Deadly E. coli

The worst bacterial infection is the potentially deadly bacteria *E. coli* 0157:H7. Regular *E. coli* is usually benign, but this mutated form of *E. coli* has potential lethal properties. It was first identified and isolated in 1982. This potentially lethal strain of the bacteria enters America's food supply in the slaughterhouses and is nearly always associated with beef, especially hamburger. The bacteria develops when chunks of manure and dirt fall from the animal's hide onto the meat as the hide is removed. If fecal material or the contents of the intestinal tract are spilled onto the meat, the meat must be thoroughly washed for it to remain uncontaminated. Unfortunately, this often does not occur. Scientists believe this particular deadly strain of E. coli mutated because of the overuse of antibiotics in today's cattle.

Perhaps the most notorious outbreak of E. coli 0157:H7 occurred in January of 1993 when a number of children were admitted to a hospital in Seattle, Washington, with bloody diarrhea. Health officials soon traced the outbreak of food poisoning to undercooked hamburgers served at several fast-food restaurants. Eventually the bacteria, E. coli 0157:H7, was isolated. In all, more than seven hundred people in four states developed food poisoning, more than two hundred were hospitalized, and four died.

The early symptoms of E. coli illness are similar to those of influenza. However, severe vomiting, diarrhea, and eventually bloody diarrhea develop if the infection is severe. A powerful toxin called the "Shiga toxin" attacks the lining of the intestines. In approximately 5 percent of cases, this toxin enters the bloodstream, causing hemolytic uremic syndrome, which eventually can lead to the shutting down of the kidneys and other vital organs, with internal bleeding causing eventual destruction of vital organs.

Young children and the elderly are especially susceptible to E. coli 0157:H7. In salmonella food poisoning, a person generally has to consume a fairly large quantity of bacteria before becoming sick—generally about a million organisms. But with E. coli 0157:H7 as few as five organisms can cause an infection.

The best protection against E. coli is to thoroughly cook ground beef and all other types of red meat. Beef, lamb, and pork (if you must insist on eating pork) should always be cooked to an internal temperature of at least 160 degrees Fahrenheit. The same knife should never be used to cut meat and then vegetables, fruits, or other foods—this leads quickly to cross-contamination. A case of this occurred in Milwaukee in the summer of 2000. More than five hundred people were ill, with sixty-two confirmed E. coli infections. The outbreak killed a three-year-old girl who had eaten watermelon at a restaurant—the melon had apparently been splattered with the juices of E. coli–contaminated sirloin tips.

According to the CDC, approximately 73,000 people a year are stricken with E. coli, and approximately 60 die from this bacteria. But when meat is slaughtered according to strict Jewish customs, E. coli is nonexistent.

Mad Cow Disease

Even more ominous than E. coli 0157:H7 is mad cow disease. This disease initially appeared in Britain in the mid-1980s and has since spread to France, Germany, Spain, Switzerland, Portugal, Belgium, Denmark, Italy, the Netherlands, Luxembourg, and Ireland. It has been found in fifteen countries in Europe and the Middle East, and at least one case has been reported in Canada.

Mad cow disease is technically known as bovine spongiform encephalopathy (BSE). It is an infectious and incurable disease that attacks the brain and nervous system of cattle. The brains of infected animals become sponge-like and full of holes, thus the name "spongiform." Animals with this disease first manifest symptoms of kicking or shaking, or making jittery or spastic movements. At times, a cow may lay on the ground shaking and mooing.

Mad cow disease is primarily the result of poor feeding practices for the cattle. As cattle have been slaughtered, part of the remains of the cattle were used to make cattle feed. Cattle are herbivores, but slaughter-houses determined that leftover brains, bones, blood, and other cattle parts from slaughtered animals could be added to cattle feed and fed to cattle in feed lots to enable them to grow larger and faster. In Britain, the remains of diseased cattle were mixed into the feed, allowing the disease to develop and spread rapidly. Mad cow disease is not caused by a virus, bacteria, or parasite, but rather by an infectious protein called a *prion*. Herbivore cattle were simply not created to consume meat products!

When sheep develop a disease caused by prions, the name of the disease is *scrapie*. That name was first given because infected sheep habitually rubbed against anything they could find, including barbed wire. Many animals literally "scraped" themselves to death.

In human beings, mad cow disease is called Creutzfeldt-Jakob disease (CJD). Human beings can contract the disease by consuming the infectious proteins of infected cattle or sheep.

In mad cow disease, scrapie, and CJD, the pattern of spongelike brains is manifested as the prions kill brain cells, producing holes in the brain tissue.

Prions cannot be destroyed except by heating them to more than 800 degrees Fahrenheit—a degree of heat that is virtually never used for any purpose. Therefore, when prions infect brain cells, the result is almost certainly fatal. There is no cure—nothing can be done to remove prions from the bodies of cattle, sheep, or infected humans.

BSE or mad cow disease, scrapie in sheep, kuru in New Guinea, and CJD in the Western world, all affect the same part of the brain and are essentially the same disease whether in man or animal. Scientists in the 1940s discovered that many people from a tribe in New Guinea were dying of a mysterious brain disease called "kuru."

The native custom in this tribe included cannibalism in which bone marrow, viscera, and brain were cooked and eaten. Natives of this tribe would eat their relatives when they died in hopes of attaining their mental and physical strengths. Kuru was geographically limited to New Guinea. CJD is the same disease process as kuru; however, it is not geographically limited and has been reported in over 50 countries throughout the world.

The first human case of this disease in Europe was diagnosed in Britain in 1996. Since then, in Europe, ninety-two people have died from mad cow disease: eighty-eight in Britain, three in France, and one in Ireland. The U.S. Department of Agriculture (USDA) has banned importing both animals and animal products from England since 1990, and from all of Europe since 1997. The USDA has also embarked on a surveillance program to test high-risk animals.

In France, more than forty thousand cows a week are tested, according to Michael Hanson, who studies prion disease at the Consumer Policy Institute. But in the U.S., only about two thousand brains out of thirty-six million cattle are tested annually. The tests are conducted after the brain of the cow has been removed so it can be examined under a microscope. The test usually takes ten days, which means the carcass from the examined animal may have already been consumed. In Europe, the tests are conducted in only four hours.

In Europe, examiners are finding prion disease even in cattle that appear healthy. That is particularly troublesome.[1]

In Britain, even though mad cow disease appears to be on the decline in cattle, the number of people being diagnosed with variant CJD is growing. The disease usually takes years to develop so we may just be seeing the tip of the iceberg.

The dietary laws given by God thousands of years ago are diametrically opposed to feeding animal parts and blood to cattle. Deadly diseases such as mad cow disease never occurred in animals in Bible times! Diseased animals would have been identified and removed from a flock or herd very quickly. This disease has been produced by man's tampering with the natural feeding practices of animals.

KOSHER MEAT VERSUS REGULAR MEAT

In 1906, Upton Sinclair wrote *The Jungle*, a book that described practices of the meat-packing industry that threatened the health of consumers. The book garnered the attention of President Theodore Roosevelt, who then became instrumental in passing legislation requiring federal inspection of all meat sold through interstate commerce. The meat-packing industry was required to foot the bill for cleaning up its own industry.

The typical kill rate in the early 1900s was about fifty cattle an hour. The slaughter rate in some of the newest plants is nearly four hundred head of cattle an hour! Most plants slaughter well over three hundred head of cattle every working hour of the week. As a nation, we are consuming far more beef per capita than anyone in ancient Israel could ever have imagined.

According to the U.S. Department of Agriculture, some 37,642,000 cattle and calves were slaughtered in 1991. Perhaps one piece of good news is that in the figures related to 1991, Americans were found to be eating less beef than they had been fifteen years earlier. In 1976, beef consumption was about ninety-four pounds of beef per person per year. In 1991, the typical American ate only about sixty-eight pounds of beef a year.[2] Even so, sixty-eight pounds of beef a year is more than a pound of hamburger per person per week on average! And many Americans eat far more than that.

The Usual Processing of Beef

Very few people I meet understand the procedures of a slaughterhouse. They are important for us to understand, however, if we truly want to eat the way Jesus ate. Let me give you a brief overview.

It takes about twenty–five minutes to turn a live steer into steaks and hamburger in our modern slaughterhouses. Working in a slaughterhouse is one of the most dangerous jobs in the United States, with an injury rate about three times higher than the rate in a typical manufacturing factory. Production lines have been speeded up to increase the volume of production and, thereby, profitability.

In a typical modern slaughterhouse, cattle walk down a narrow chute in single file until they reach a "knocker." The knocker is a worker who fires a bolt gun with a retractable metal rod into the steer's forehead. The shot must be precise for it to knock the animal unconscious. There is a high failure rate among many beef plants that use this type of gun—in fact, only 36 percent of slaughterhouses using it earned a rating of acceptable, which means the cattle were knocked unconscious with a single blow at least 95 percent of the time. Many times an animal has to receive a second or third blow with a bolt gun.

When the steer falls, one of its hind legs is shackled to a chain that lifts the animal into the air where it is ready to be bled and butchered by workers on down the production line. A worker uses a long knife to slit the neck of the steer, severing its carotid arteries. The long knife must hit the exact spot to kill the animal humanely. Often, animals wake up (since they were never really knocked unconscious) and begin moving their heads or twisting and arching their backs; at other times, workers use unsharpened knives due to their production quotas. An animal can get seven minutes down the production line and still be alive. Some, in fact, are still alive as the hide is being stripped off them.[3]

Animals are skinned and dismembered within minutes of having their throats cut, and since some animals are still alive at this point in the

59

process, they literally are killed "piece by piece." The fear and pain in animals still alive produce hormones that can damage the meat. Also, fear in an animal still alive causes the muscles of the animal to contract and arteries to be constricted—this enables the animal to hold blood in its tissues and meat.

The saying "if slaughterhouses were made of glass, we would all be vegetarians" is certainly true!

The Slaughter That Is Biblical

The slaughter of animals in the Bible was quite different from what goes on today. First, animals were not killed in any kind of "processing plant" mode. There was no assembly-line approach. It was the common procedure for one animal to be selected from a flock or herd as described in Deuteronomy 12:21: "You may slaughter from your herd and from your flock which the LORD has given you."

The actual method of slaughter is known as the *shehitah*. Jews consider this method to have been given to Moses as part of the "oral Torah"—the verbal law that God gave to Moses on Mount Sinai. Moses revealed this oral law to the religious heads of Israel, who in turn handed it down from generation to generation by word of mouth. The oral Torah was finally written as part of the Talmud in the second century.

The *shehitah* method of slaughter was intended to cause the least amount of pain to an animal, and to result in the extraction of the most amount of blood. The animal's throat was to be cut rapidly with a to-and-fro cut. The movement was intended to take only a fraction of a second and resulted in the severing of the trachea, esophagus, two vagus nerves, both carotid arteries, and the jugular vein. The blade of the knife was to be adequately long and was to be kept extremely sharp and free of any nick or irregularity.

An animal's neck was to be clean and free of mud, pebbles, dirt, and sand prior to its being killed. The cut was to be made without any hesitation, with a continuous stroke, and with no pressure applied—the sharpness of the blade did the cutting.

After the cut was made, the cut was to be examined by the slaughterer, who was called the *shochet*, to make sure the trachea and esophagus had been properly and thoroughly severed. The process is one that requires significant skill and expertise—it was also to be done with piety and respect for the fact that God had created the animal that was being killed. Slaughtermen had to pass a rigid exam and be certified by Rabbinic authorities.

If any of these procedures were not followed, the meat was to be considered unfit for consumption.

After the slaughter, the animal's lungs and other internal organs were examined. Animals that have been injured in a fall, or that have been torn by wild animals or poisoned, will generally have a defect in their internal organs. Such animals were considered unfit for consumption.

Using this biblical method, no animal suffered more than necessary. No harmful hormones were released into the tissues and meat. The maximum amount of blood was drained from the animal.

What About Veal?

In raising veal calves in America today, a calf is usually allowed to nurse only one or two days before it is removed from its mother. It is then locked in a small stall and given a high-calorie diet absent of iron—this keeps the calf anemic and results in the pale color and tender texture of veal meat. Antibiotics are used to keep the calf from becoming ill. Many veal calves develop lung adhesions. They would certainly not pass the test of a *shochet*.

KOSHER MEAT IS DRAINED OF BLOOD

As we have noted previously, the Levitical Law forbids the eating of blood, even if it comes from clean animals. Leviticus 7:26–27 says clearly, "You shall not eat any blood in any of your dwellings, whether of bird or beast. Whoever eats any blood, that person shall be cut off from his people."

Kosher beef has been thoroughly drained of all blood. How exactly is this to be done? Two methods are used.

The first method of koshering is a "soak and salt" method. This is actually the method that gives definition to the word *kosher*. In this process, meat is thoroughly washed under cold running water, and then the meat is immersed in cool water for thirty minutes. After the soaking, the meat is covered on all sides by a layer of medium coarse salt, which helps absorb blood from the meat. The meat is placed on a surface at an incline so the blood will drain. It is kept in salt for one hour, and then thoroughly rinsed again under running water. The meat is heavily rinsed three times or undergoes three thorough soakings, each time in clean water. The triple rinsing and soaking remove all salt and blood.[4]

The other method of koshering is by broiling. In this method, raw meat is thoroughly washed and lightly salted. It is then placed on a grill and broiled—this method allows the blood to drain away as the meat is cooked. The meat may be turned over so it broils evenly. After the meat is broiled, it is rinsed with cool water to wash away any residual blood that may remain on the surface of the meat.

Many supermarkets offer kosher meats. Again, the price may be a little higher, but your health is worth it.

THE PROBLEM OF GLUTTONY

Gluttony is not simply eating large quantities of food. Gluttony from a biblical standpoint also involves eating the wrong kinds of food.

We read in Proverbs:

> When you sit down to eat with a ruler,
>
> Consider carefully what is before you;
>
> And put a knife to your throat
>
> If you are a man given to appetite.
>
> Do not desire his delicacies,
>
> For they are deceptive food. (23:1–3)

The food of the rich is described in several places in the Bible as "delicacies." These were foods rich in fat, including fatty meat.

The eating of meat in the Scriptures is regularly associated with gluttony. For example, the daily provision of meat in King Solomon's court included "ten fatted oxen, twenty oxen from the pastures, one hundred sheep, besides deer, gazelles, roebucks, and fatted fowl" (1 Kings 4:23). This volume of meat was considered excessive by those who wrote of Solomon—the meat was a sign of his overburdening the productivity of the land for his own political purposes and personal luxury.

The Bible takes a strong stance against gluttony—the routine practice of overeating:

> Hear, my son, and be wise;
>
> And guide your heart in the way.
>
> Do not mix with winebibbers,
>
> Or with gluttonous eaters of meat;

For the drunkard and the glutton will come to poverty,

And drowsiness will clothe a man with rags. (Prov. 23:19–21)

The penalty for gluttony in the Law of Moses is severe. Excessive drinking and gluttony were hallmarks of those who were "stubborn and rebellious" (See Deut. 21:20). Because of this, the punishment for those who were stubborn and rebellious was death by stoning! (v. 21).

Throughout their history, the Jews have regarded those who overate and drank excessively to be people who were selfish, self-indulgent, and undisciplined. These character traits are opposite of the godly character qualities of restraint, self-control, and generosity toward others.

Gluttony in the Wilderness

In Numbers 11, we find an interesting story about the children of Israel. As they wandered in the wilderness, they complained and murmured about their daily provision of manna. We are told in Numbers 11:4 that the multitude began asking, "Who will give us meat to eat?" This question arose because the people "yielded to craving."

God answered their craving this way:

A wind went out from the LORD, and it brought quail from the sea and left them fluttering near the camp, about a day's journey on this side and about a day's journey on the other side, all around the camp, and about two cubits above the surface of the ground. And the people stayed up all that day, all that night, and all the next day, and gathered the quail (he who gathered least gathered ten homers); and they spread them out for themselves all around the camp. But while the meat was still between their teeth, before it was chewed, the wrath of the LORD was aroused against the people, and the LORD struck the people with a very great plague. So he called the name of that place Kibroth

Hattaavah, because there they buried the peop craving. (Num. 11:31–34)

Notice that the person who gathered th gathered ten homers' worth—that's more than one . quail!

The clear message of this passage is not that the people died because they ate birds, but because they had a gluttonous spirit, and because they "yielded to craving."

FOUR THINGS WE SHOULD DO

If red meat is going to be eaten, I strongly recommend that my patients and clients do the following:

1. Cut down on the intake of animal protein. Eat far fewer portions of red meat per month.

2. Make sure all the red meat that you do eat is trimmed of fat. Choose "extra lean" and "range-fed" meats, and if possible, choose kosher meat.

3. Store the meat in the coldest part of the refrigerator, and use it within two to five days of purchase. Ground beef and sausage should be tossed out after two days. Frozen meats should be defrosted in a refrigerator.

4. Cook ground beef to temperatures of at least 160 degrees Fahrenheit. Cooked meats should not be left outside the refrigerator for longer than two hours. If you are having a cookout or a picnic, make sure that any leftover hamburger patties are refrigerated as soon as possible. If they are left out for even a few hours, the bacteria multiples

apidly! Be sure to reheat all leftovers that include meats to their proper temperature. That includes heating pizza to 160 degrees Fahrenheit.[5]

POULTRY AND EGGS

The Law of Moses gave very specific instructions about the consumption of fowl:

> And these you shall regard as an abomination among the birds; they shall not be eaten, they are an abomination: the eagle, the vulture, the buzzard, the kite, and the falcon after its kind; every raven after its kind, the ostrich, the short-eared owl, the seagull, and the hawk after its kind; the little owl, the fisher owl, and the screech owl; the white owl, the jackdaw, and the carrion vulture; the stork, the heron after its kind, the hoopoe, and the bat. (Lev. 11:13–19)

Twenty-four types of birds are identified in Leviticus, chiefly birds of prey. In Deuteronomy 14:13–15 we find the phrases "after its kind" and "after their kinds" associated with several of the bird species, although no overriding description of the forbidden birds is given.

Deuteronomy 14:20 states, "You may eat all clean birds." These birds included chicken, geese, turkeys, ducks, and doves.[6]

During the time of Jesus, Jews consumed domestic fowl such as chickens, geese, pigeons, partridges, duck, and quail. We do not have specific references for Jesus eating poultry. He did, however, refer to chicks and hens in a statement recorded in Matthew 23:37:

> O Jerusalem, Jerusalem, the one who kills the prophets and stones those who are sent to her! How often I wanted to gather your children

together, as a hen gathers her chicks under her wings, but you were not willing!

The laws related to the slaughtering of red meat also applied to the slaughter of fowl. Koshering of fowl meat was performed by broiling, soaking, and salting.

THE PROBLEM WITH OUR POULTRY TODAY

Today, chickens, like beef, are usually given steroids, growth hormones, and antibiotics. Chickens and eggs are both carriers of drug-resistant strains of salmonella, staphylococcus, and campylobacter bacteria. These are pathogenic bacteria that are commonly associated with food poisoning.

Chickens are routinely housed in overcrowded conditions where they get very little exercise, and the result is a rise in the fat content of the meat. Organic, free-range chickens and kosher chickens are raised primarily on grain and grasses, and are kept free of hormones, antibiotics, and pesticides. They are significantly lower in fat than chickens raised in our nation's "chicken factories."

In 1992, the consumption of chicken surpassed the consumption of beef in America.[7] The added benefit to Americans is that a pound of chicken costs about half as much as a pound of beef.

WHAT ABOUT EATING EGGS?

Eggs were also consumed during Bible times. The use of eggs was actually fairly common during the time of Jesus.

One of the most interesting questions asked in the book of Job is this: "Is there any taste in the white of an egg?" The speaker goes on to say, "My soul refuses to touch them; they are as loathsome food to me" (Job 6:6–7).

Jesus, however, put eggs in a more positive light. He placed them in the category of good gifts when He taught:

Ask, and it will be given to you; seek, and you will find; knock, and it will be opened to you . . . If a son . . . asks for an egg, will he offer him a scorpion? If you then, being evil, know how to give good gifts to your children, how much more will your heavenly Father give the Holy Spirit to those who ask Him! (Luke 11:9, 11–13)

Eggs were prepared in several ways, including boiling and frying. Some people cooked fish under a layer of eggs.

I recommend that you purchase eggs from free-range chickens. Free-range chickens, as noted before, are not given hormones, antibiotics, or pesticides, and they usually feed on grass or grain—all of these factors enhance the nutritional value of the egg.

If a blood spot is found on a fertilized egg, that is possibly a sign that a chicken embryo has started to form. Eggs that have blood spots are forbidden under kosher food laws.

Many people avoid eggs because they fear a problem with cholesterol. Actually, egg yolks are one of the best-known sources for choline, which is the raw material used in the body's production of acetylcholine, one of the most important neurotransmitters associated with brain function and memory. In addition to choline, eggs contain folic acid, B vitamins, antioxidants, and unsaturated fats.

What most people don't understand is that egg yolks are high in lecithin—an agent that emulsifies, or breaks up, the cholesterol of the egg yolk. A study out of Harvard University in April 1999 showed that eating one egg a day is unlikely to increase one's risk of (ease or strokes. In fact, consuming one egg a day may even vent heart disease.[8]

The best way to avoid the pathogenic bacteria that tend to be associated with eggs is to make sure that you eat cooked eggs. I recommend that you never add raw eggs to a health drink or shake. I also recommend that you avoid Caesar salad dressings that are made with raw eggs. If a recipe calls for a raw egg, it's best to substitute pasteurized egg whites, such as Egg Beaters.

Make sure you cook the egg until the yolk is firm. Those who eat their eggs sunny-side up, over easy, or with a yolk that is runny are at a higher risk of salmonella.

Eggs should be stored in the coldest part of the refrigerator and kept in their original containers. Do not keep eggs for more than three weeks.

FIVE THINGS WE SHOULD DO

There are several changes many of us need to make when it comes to eating poultry and eggs. Here are five things we should do in this area:

1. Limit the portion of poultry to four ounces and choose white meat over dark meat. Many people replace red meat with chicken, which is good.

2. Choose free-range chicken.

3. Remove all skin and fat from chicken.

4. Bake, grill, or roast chicken rather than cooking it in fat by frying or deep-frying it.

5. Limit consumption of eggs to no more than three or four eggs a week.

WHAT WOULD JESUS EAT?

Jesus ate clean, kosher meats—free-range animals slaughtered in a biblical way, drained of blood, and stripped of excess fat. Jesus ate red meat very sparingly. He also ate eggs and clean poultry—again, stripped of excess fat and eaten sparingly.

We can follow His example in choosing to limit our consumption of red meat, choosing free-range and kosher beef and poultry, removing all fat before cooking, and cooking our meat products by baking, grilling, or roasting and draining all the fat. We should limit our egg consumption and choose to purchase eggs from free-range chickens.

CHAPTER FIVE

OTHER FORMS OF PROTEIN THAT JESUS ATE

ONE OF THE FIRST STATEMENTS THAT GOD MADE TO
Moses from a burning bush was this:

> I have come down to deliver them [the Israelites] out of the hand of the
> Egyptians, and to bring them up from that land to a good and large land,
> to a land flowing with milk and honey. (Ex. 3:8)

Most people who have read that phrase know that a "land flowing
with milk and honey" was considered to be a blessing, but they don't fully
appreciate what the phrase means. A land "flowing with milk" was a land
with such lush pasturelands that the cattle, sheep, and goats could graze
to their heart's delight, and in so doing produce an abundance of milk. A
land "flowing with honey" was a land with such lush flowering vegetation, including fruit trees, that the blossoms provided abundant nectar
for honeybees. Most of us would enjoy living in such a land!

What happened to the milk produced by the flocks envisioned by the ancient Israelites? Most of it was used to nurture baby calves and lambs. Some of it was used for human consumption. The Israelites used cow's milk (Isa. 28:9), goat's milk (Prov. 27:27), sheep's milk (Deut. 32:14), and camel's milk (Gen. 32:15). Certainly human babies were fed with the mother's breast milk or the milk from a wet nurse whenever possible.

The milk used by the Israelites was generally consumed in the form of butter, cheese, or yogurt. We read in Deuteronomy 32:14 about "curds from the cattle, and milk of the flock." In Proverbs 30:33, we read that "the churning of milk produces butter." Cheese is mentioned in 1 Samuel 17:18. Jesse, the father of David, gave him ten cheeses to take to the captain of the Israelite army.

Many Bible scholars believe that the "butter" of the Bible was actually a type of curdled milk, cultured in a way very similar to yogurt. Curdled milk, in some translations, also refers to cheese.[1]

While people in Jesus' time consumed some butter, cheese, and yogurt, it is unlikely that they ever actually drank milk. Are you aware that the human being is the only mammal that continues to drink milk as an adult? Other animals, it seems, are smarter than we are in that regard. Only their young drink milk—which is important to the building of tissues.

THE HIGH-FAT CONTENT OF MILK

Butter, milk, and cheese are all high in saturated fat. Butter contains 81 percent fat. Cheese typically has about 75 percent saturated fat. Whole milk, even though it contains only 4 percent saturated fat, draws 48 percent of its calories from that fat.

Eating saturated fats from dairy products raises LDL (bad) cholesterol levels. Conversely, decreasing or avoiding dairy fat and eliminating fatty cuts of meat from the diet nearly always result in lower LDL (bad) cholesterol.

Pasteurization and Homogenization

Whole milk is processed by pasteurization, which requires the milk to be heated to 160 degrees Fahrenheit for forty-five minutes to kill harmful bacteria. But the process also kills beneficial bacteria. Pasteurization denatures the enzymes in milk and alters the structure of protein, which may be a reason some people are allergic to dairy products. Furthermore, pasteurization decreases the ability of the calcium in milk to be absorbed.

In addition to pasteurization, whole milk is processed by homogenization. This process breaks down the butter fat into many tiny droplets that are too small to rise to the top of milk. The tiny fat droplets produced by homogenization are able to pass easily into the bloodstream, whereas butter fat droplets in nonhomogenized fat are not absorbed nearly as well. Therefore, a much higher percentage of fat in homogenized milk enters the bloodstream, which results in a rise in triglycerides and cholesterol.

Because of the increased absorption of the small fat particles in homogenized milk, an enzyme in the butter fat called xanthine oxidase is able to damage the smooth lining of blood vessels, which paves the way for a buildup of plaque in a person's arteries. Countless degenerative diseases are related to increased triglycerides and increased plaque formation.

Butter

Butter was a very rare commodity in Jesus' time, in part because butter requires refrigeration. For the most part, the butter in Jesus' time was olive oil, not our milk-based butter.

If you choose to eat butter, I recommend that you mix equal parts of olive oil with butter. The best way to do this is to melt the butter and then add the olive oil. Return the mixture to the refrigerator to harden it. Use it sparingly.

THE BENEFITS OF SKIM AND NONFAT MILK

While fatty, whole milk is certainly not for adults, skim or nonfat milk may be. Researchers at Vanderbilt University found that skim milk seemed to lower the liver's output of LDL (bad) cholesterol. The calcium in skim milk may also have beneficial effects on high blood pressure and mild hypertension.

Just one cup of milk has these minerals:

Calcium	250 milligrams
Protein	8.4 grams
Potassium	406 milligrams
Sodium	126 milligrams

Here are some health benefits of milk:

· The calcium in milk builds bones in children and may help prevent or slow the development of osteoporosis in older women.

· The calcium in milk may help lower high blood pressure.

· The high calcium and vitamin D content of milk helps prevent colon cancer.

Despite these benefits, those who have a milk allergy, milk sensitivity, or milk intolerance should avoid milk products, or only consume them periodically. I personally recommend soy milk in place of regular milk. However, if you must drink milk, choose skim milk.

CHEESE AND YOGURT

Since milk could not be stored in biblical times, it had to be fermented to keep it from spoiling. The cheese, butter, and yogurt mentioned in the Bible were made from fermented milk from cows, goats, camels, and sheep.

The prophet Isaiah foretold a day when the king of Assyria and his troops would descend upon the Israelites. Isaiah said in that day:

A young man will keep alive a young cow and two sheep;
So it shall be, from the abundance of milk they give,
That he will eat curds;
For curds and honey everyone will eat who is left in the land. (Isa. 7:21–22)

Curds, in this passage, refers to cheese or thick yogurt.

CHEESE IN BIBLE TIMES

Cheese in Bible times often had garlic, parsley, thyme, dill, and olive oil added to it. This is something you can make today:

Start with a half pound of fresh curd cheese (or farmer's cheese, cream cheese, or yogurt cheese). I recommend fat-free cream cheese or yogurt cheese. Add four cloves of garlic, two tablespoons of olive oil, and a tablespoon each of thyme, dill, and fresh parsley. If you don't have fresh herbs, use only one teaspoon each of dried thyme, dill, and parsley. Add salt to taste. This mixture is excellent on nutty, whole-grain breads.

By the way, you may be interested to know that it takes about a gallon of milk to produce a half pound of cheese. That's one of the reasons cheese is so much more expensive than milk.

I recommend that you limit your consumption of both butter and cheese to special occasions.

YOGURT IS A "SUPER FOOD"

Yogurt is the most healthy of the dairy foods. It is a cultured dairy product in which milk has been inoculated with bacteria that ferment the milk sugar into lactic acid. Yogurt contains lactobacillus acidophilus and other friendly bacteria, as well as vitamins A and B. In choosing yogurt, it is best to choose nonfat, plain yogurt that does not have any sugar, fruit, or artificial flavor or color added. You can always add your own fresh fruit to yogurt to improve the flavor. The yogurt should contain live cultures of bacteria, especially lactobacillus acidophilus and bifidobacterium. You can generally find this kind of yogurt at a health food store.

Yogurt is highly regarded around the world as a "super food."

It seems to be a mainstay in the diets of people who are traditionally long-lived, such as those living in parts of Turkey, Armenia, and remote regions of the Caucasus Mountains.

Yogurt is high in bone-building calcium. It has been linked to the prevention of colds, allergies, and cancer. It helps prevent dangerous intestinal infections and improves bowel function.

Here is what a person will get in a single cup of low-fat plain yogurt:

Calories	144
Cholesterol	14 milligrams
Carbohydrates	16 grams
Fat	3.5 grams

Protein	11.9 grams
Calcium	415 milligrams
Sodium	159 milligrams
Potassium	531 milligrams

Fruit-flavored yogurt, by comparison, can have 225 or more calories in a single cup.

A very popular salad in the Middle East is yogurt based. To two cups of plain yogurt, add two tablespoons minced fresh mint (or two teaspoons dried mint), two cloves of crushed garlic, and two large cucumbers (sliced). The yogurt mixture is sometimes served on a bed of watercress and sliced radishes.

You certainly may eat low-fat, plain yogurt with live cultures more frequently than you eat cheese or butter.

THE PROTEIN SOURCE NOT AVAILABLE TO JESUS

One of the major sources of high-quality protein from the plant world is the soybean. Unfortunately, soybeans were not available in Israel at the time of Jesus. Had they been, I feel certain that Jesus would have eaten them regularly.

The soybean is native to China and has been cultivated there for more than thirteen thousand years. It is the most widely grown and used bean in the world.

The soybean is an important crop in the United States, ranking above wheat, corn, and cotton. However, it is mainly used for its oil and for animal feed.

The amino acid profile in soy is comparable to protein in animal food. One acre of soybean plants can provide nearly twenty times the amount of protein as in cattle grazed on that same amount of land. Soybeans are packed with phytonutrients that are powerful protectors against cancers.

The Japanese consume thirty to fifty times more soy products than Americans do.[2] The Japanese have approximately a quarter of the incidences of breast and prostate cancer we have in the United States. Soybeans contain phytoestrogens, otherwise known as isoflavones, which bind to estrogen receptors. The result is a much weaker estrogenic effect, which in turn decreases the risk of developing breast cancer. This same effect helps reduce the incidence of prostate cancer in men. Soybeans also contain protease inhibitors, which have been shown to inhibit the growth of other kinds of cancers in animals.

Soy is effective in helping lower cholesterol levels, thereby helping prevent heart disease.

Soy has been shown to help prevent osteoporosis as well as to help control hot flashes in menopausal women. Soy products are high in calcium, and this, in addition to the high levels of the phytoestrogen genistein in soy, helps prevent bone loss in postmenopausal women. Soy foods and soy supplements are important in controlling the hot flashes and vaginal dryness associated with menopause. Soy may also be effective in controlling the symptoms of PMS.

Soy is available in many different forms, including miso—which is fermented soy paste. Miso is frequently used in making Oriental soups. Other common forms of soy on the market are tofu (soybean curd), soy flour, soy nuts, soy protein mixes, soy milk, and tempeh (fermented soybeans). Supplements of isoflavones and genistein can also be purchased directly at health food stores.

Other Plant Proteins

Many other plants can contribute to our supply of protein, although for the most part, these plants have incomplete protein. Various beans and legumes need to be combined with whole grains to produce a complete protein.

HOW MUCH PROTEIN?

How much protein do we need a day? The average adult needs about 0.8 grams of protein per kilogram (2.2 pounds). In other words, for the average 154-pound person (70K), 56 grams of protein are needed. Infants and children have higher protein requirements based on body weight than adults, and elderly adults need less. Many Americans, however, are routinely eating 100 to 200 grams of protein a day, generally in the form of meat!

One of the best things we can do for our health is to lower our overall consumption of protein. We can do this best by lowering our consumption of meat, relying on more plant sources for protein.

Jesus ate a balanced diet, and I have no doubt that He also ate a balance of proteins from a variety of sources. Our bodies need protein; they do not, however, need an overdose of protein.

WHAT WOULD JESUS EAT?

Jesus ate yogurt, and some cheese and butter, generally on special occasions. In His day, dairy products fell mostly into the category of condiments rather than main dishes or beverages.

We should limit our consumption of dairy to nonfat and low-fat products, especially yogurt with live cultures. We should eat butter and cheese sparingly and rarely.

CHAPTER SIX

THE VEGETABLES
THAT JESUS
ATE

As I STATED IN AN EARLIER CHAPTER, GOD'S INITIAL
plan for mankind was for men and women to be vegetarians. In the very
first book of the Bible, God said, "See, I have given you every herb that
yields seed which is on the face of all the earth, and every tree whose
fruit yields seed; to you it shall be for food" (Gen. 1:29).

God's plan was also for the other creatures He made to be vegetarian.
He said, "'Also, to every beast of the earth, to every bird of the air, and
to everything that creeps on the earth, in which there is life, I have given
every green herb for food'; and it was so" (Gen. 1:30).

The only vegetation that was off limits to man and woman was the "tree
of the knowledge of good and evil" (Gen. 2:17). God's command was that
Adam and Eve could eat of every other tree of the Garden except that tree.

After Adam and Eve rebelled against God, they were driven from the
Garden, and the ground was cursed. Adam and Eve were told this about
the earth:

Both thorns and thistles it shall bring forth for you,
And you shall eat the herb of the field. (Gen. 3:18)

Adam tilled the ground. The vegetarian period of the Bible lasted from the time of Adam to the time of Noah, and during this vegetarian period, the people had much longer life spans than they did in later eras.

Was Jesus a vegetarian? No. We know that He frequently consumed fish. We also know that He ate lamb at the Passover Feast. It is likely that He ate other meats as well during feast times and on special occasions, such as weddings.

Did Jesus eat vegetables? Absolutely. We have no direct reference to this, but vegetables were the mainstay of the diet during Bible times.

With the exception of the manna-eating years in the wilderness, the Israelites have always eaten a diet loaded with a wide variety of vegetables, herbs, and plant-based spices.

Numbers 11:5 tells us that the Israelites craved these foods from Egypt: cucumbers, melons, leeks, onions, and garlic, as well as the abundance of fish available to them in Egypt. We should note that these foods were not bad for the Israelites simply because they were Egyptian foods—rather, these were foods that were customarily a part of the Israelites' diet while they lived in Egypt, and they were, therefore, foods they missed as they wandered in the desert wilderness.

The fact is, these foods—cucumbers, melons, leeks, onions, and garlic—were very healthy foods, totally approved by God in the dietary laws given to Moses.

Let's take a look at some of the major vegetables consumed in Jesus' day.

BEANS AND LENTILS

Beans, peas, and lentils are easily cultivated, and in Bible times, they were used to make purees, pottages, or when mixed with millet, a coarse bread. They were easily dried and stored.

The story of Esau and Jacob is one of the most powerful stories in Genesis. We are told that Esau had been out in the field hunting all day and came home very hungry, to the point of feeling faint. (He may have been suffering from low blood sugar!) Esau smelled a pot of soup cooking, and he said to his brother, Jacob, "Please feed me with that same red stew, for I am weary" (Gen. 25:30).

Red stew is a very ancient dish in the Middle East. It is made of beans and lentils boiled in garlic—a very tasty, aromatic, and nutritious meal. Jacob capitalized on his brother's hunger and said, "Sell me your birthright as of this day" (Gen. 25:31).

In biblical times, the firstborn son enjoyed a favored position that was his solely because of his birth order. This birthright gave Esau the privilege of inheriting a double portion of his father's assets; he was also expecting a special blessing before his father died so that he might fully use that inheritance to its maximum advantage. A firstborn son's birthright also meant that he became the head of the family upon the death of his father.

A father could not transfer the birthright to another child, but a firstborn son could forfeit his rights. Esau did just that. He said, "Look, I am about to die; so what profit is this birthright to me?" (Gen. 25:32). Jacob replied, "Swear to me as of this day" (v. 33). And Esau swore to him and sold his birthright to Jacob. In return, Jacob gave Esau "bread and a stew of lentils" (v. 34).

As a result, all Jews became descendants of Jacob rather than Esau. Simply because a pot of beans was so tempting to a man who had little regard for his own destiny!

THE HIGH HEALTH VALUE OF BEANS

Beans are loaded with soluble fiber, which helps lower LDL (bad) cholesterol and reduces blood pressure.

Dr. James Anderson, a noted researcher at the University of Kentucky, recommends a minimum of one cup of cooked beans daily to help prevent heart disease. He has found in his research that middle-aged men who were fed a diet that included beans dramatically reduced their cholesterol levels by as much as 19 percent. A similar study at the University of Minnesota mirrored these results when subjects ate one cup of cooked dried beans daily instead of sugar, bread, and potatoes.

The fiber in beans also helps to keep blood sugar levels stable, fights off hunger, and has been shown to reduce the insulin requirements of diabetics. Beans can help prevent constipation and the development of hemorrhoids and other bowel-related problems. Diets high in beans will help to lower one's risk of developing certain cancers.

Beans and garlic have often been boiled together to produce a primitive version of cough medicine.

Even canned beans have some therapeutic benefit. I do not recommend canned beans, however, because they tend to be high in salt. But if you absolutely must have canned beans, first rinse them in clean water to remove some of the salt.

Beans are packed with vitamin C, which has great antioxidant value. Just one cup of beans can provide

· 6 to 7 grams of fiber

· potassium, iron, and thiamine

· 12 grams of complex carbohydrates or starches

· 17.9 grams of protein

And that cup of beans has no cholesterol and virtually no fat.

You'll note from the breakdown that beans are a food high in protein. They usually provide two to four times more protein than grains. They have been called "the poor man's meat."

In 597 B.C., King Jehoiachin surrendered Jerusalem to the Babylonian army and was taken into exile. Taken with the king were approximately ten thousand men—soldiers, craftsmen, statesmen, and religious leaders. Among those men was Ezekiel, the prophet. Ezekiel declared God's messages to those who were living in exile. He saw himself as a "lookout"— a person who needed to give warning of approaching or impending danger. He was also something of an actor. God frequently commanded him to dramatize, or act out, his messages so they could be readily seen and understood by the exiled Israelites.

In Ezekiel 4, the Lord commanded Ezekiel to lie on his left side for 390 days, and when he was finished, the Lord directed him to lie on his right side for 40 days. The prophet represented Israel as he lay on his left side (Israel was the northern kingdom), and he represented Judah as he lay on his right side (Judah was the southern kingdom). The length of time Ezekiel lay on each side represented the length of time Israel and Judah were going to be punished for their sin.

God said to Ezekiel, "Also take for yourself wheat, barley, beans, lentils, millet, and spelt [or rye]; put them into one vessel, and make bread of them for yourself" (Ezek. 4:9). Ezekiel was to eat this bread in the amount of twenty shekels over a day, along with water. That was about half a pound of bread. The Lord also commanded him to eat barley cakes that were baked over a fire that used human waste as fuel. (See Ezek. 4:12.)

Note that Ezekiel lived on this bread for a total of 430 days! The bread was a combination of grains (wheat, barley, millet, and spelt, or rye) and legumes and beans. It was a complete-protein mixture.

Ezekiel's bread can be found in many health food stores. Some of these products are sprouted breads, which are even more nutritious. When a seed is sprouted into a new plant, the new sprouts are very nutrient rich. The protein content usually increases between 15 and 30 percent. The chlorophyll and fiber content also increases, and the sprout is usually a rich green color. Both the B vitamins and vitamin C are increased, and the sprouts contain living enzymes.

Here is a modern-day recipe for Ezekiel's bread.

EZEKIEL BREAD
A RECIPE FROM THE OLD TESTAMENT

2 ½ cups whole wheat

1 ½ cups whole rye

½ cup barley

¼ cup millet

¼ cup lentils

2 Tbsp. great northern beans (uncooked)

2 Tbsp. red kidney beans (uncooked)

2 Tbsp. pinto beans (uncooked)

2 cups lukewarm water, divided

½ cup plus 1 tsp. honey, divided

2 Tbsp. yeast

¼ cup extra-virgin olive oil

Measure and combine all the above ingredients in a large bowl. Put this mixture into a flour mill, and grind. The flour should be the consistency of regular flour. Course flour may cause digestion problems. This makes eight cups of flour. Use four cups per batch of bread.

Measure four cups of flour into a large bowl. Store the remaining flour mixture in the freezer for future use.

Measure one cup lukewarm (110–115 degrees) water in a small mixing bowl. Add one teaspoon of the honey and the yeast. Stir to dissolve the yeast. Cover and set aside, allowing the yeast to rise for five to ten minutes.

In a small mixing bowl, combine the following: olive oil, 1/2 cup honey, and remaining cup of warm water. Mix well, and add this to the flour mixture in the large bowl. Add the yeast to the bowl and stir until well mixed. The mixture should be the consistency of slightly "heavy" cornbread. Spread the mixture evenly in an 11- by 15-inch pan sprayed with no-cholesterol cooking oil. Let the mixture rise for one hour in a warm place.

Bake at 375 degrees for approximately thirty minutes. Check for doneness. Bread should be the consistency of baked cornbread.

Source: *The Bible Cure*, by Reginald Cherry (Lake Mary, Florida: Creation House 1998)

Lentils

Lentils were commonly consumed in Israel during biblical times. Lentils are actually one of the oldest cultivated plants. Archaeological evidence indicates that they were cultivated in the Near East as early as 18,000 B.C.

Lentils have 7.5 percent protein, but they are deficient in the amino acids methionine and cysteine. They are very low in fat and contain high amounts of soluble fiber that help to lower cholesterol and control blood sugar.

Lentils are good in combination with other vegetables in soups, stews, and casseroles. (Note that the recipe provided for Ezekiel's bread uses lentils.)

Garbanzo Beans

Another popular bean common to the Middle East is the garbanzo bean, also called the "chickpea." Chickpeas should be soaked overnight in the refrigerator, and the following day, the water should be discarded. I believe chickpeas are best when boiled for about an hour and then ground up in a food processor. To the garbanzo bean mix, tahina, garlic juice, garlic, salt, pepper, and cumin can be added to make what is called *hummus*. (A recipe is provided in the last chapter of the book.)

Hummus has a cake-batter-like consistency. In Israel, people usually eat hummus by dipping a piece of flat bread (pita bread) into a shallow bowl of the mixture. Olive oil is sometimes added in small quantities. Hummus has been called "the peanut butter of the Middle East."

Chickpeas are also used to make *falafel* (Middle Eastern meatballs) as well as many other dishes.

Other Beans

Bible scholars believe that many of the beans mentioned in the Bible were broad beans. Other types of beans that are highly nutritious are lima beans, green peas, black-eyed peas, white beans, navy beans, black beans, and kidney beans. All of these beans are high in soluble fiber and high in protein, but low in the amino acids cysteine and methionine.

PREPARING AND EATING BEANS

Dried beans are best prepared by soaking them overnight in twice the amount of water as beans, and then stored in the refrigerator. The water that is used for soaking the beans should be thrown away.

Many people are reluctant to eat beans because they cause excessive amounts of gas. By soaking beans overnight and then discarding the water, the gas-producing effects of beans are decreased.

Beans and brown rice can be cooked together in a Crock-Pot, with garlic, onions, and other spices. This makes a delicious, nutritious, easy-to-prepare, high-protein meal.

GARLIC, ONIONS, AND LEEKS

Garlic, onions, and leeks—all technically members of the lily family—are closely related. They have been used in both cooking and medicine for thousands of years.

GARLIC HAS POTENT HEALTH BENEFITS

Garlic was used by the Israelites as food and medicine long before Moses led the children of Israel out of Egypt. In fact, depictions of garlic bulbs have been discovered on the walls of Egyptian tombs that date back to 3200 B.C., centuries before Joseph rose to a leadership position in Egypt. Garlic is credited with having given strength to pyramid builders and courage to the Roman legions. It was used in both world wars as a potent antiseptic.

The Chinese have been using garlic for its medicinal qualities for at least three thousand years. The father of medicine, Hippocrates, used garlic, as did Aristotle. Although he is not widely known for his research into garlic, Louis Pasteur actually confirmed that garlic could kill bacteria.

At least sixty-seven different varieties of garlic and onions have been identified as growing in the Middle East. The Jewish Talmud goes so far as to specify that several types of foods are to be seasoned with garlic regularly.

The ingredient that gives garlic its strong smell—allicin—is what gives garlic its potent antibiotic properties. In hundreds of scientific experiments, allicin extract from raw garlic has been shown to destroy the germs that spread such diseases as botulism, diarrhea, dysentery, staph, tuberculosis, and typhoid. Garlic has the broadest spectrum of antimicrobial substance known in the natural world. It is an antibacterial, antifungal, antiparasitic, antiprotozoan, and antiviral.

Garlic has many different health benefits, including a number of benefits to the cardiovascular system.

Japanese scientists have distilled an antibiotic medication called kyolic from raw garlic. Kyolic has also been used to fight influenza—including a severe outbreak in Moscow in the 1950s—as well as to ward off pneumonia, whooping cough, and various intestinal disorders. Researchers are speculating that one of the reasons garlic is such an effective medicine is because it boosts the body's natural immunity.

Studies have shown that garlic appears to help slow blood coagulation, and it has antioxidant properties. It also seems to have mild antihypertensive effects and may lower cholesterol levels. Garlic has been shown to reduce both systolic and diastolic blood pressure. A number of studies have reported that patients using garlic were able to reduce their high blood pressure to manageable levels without using drugs. These anticoagulant, antioxidant, and antihypertensive properties, taken together, make garlic a good ally in preventing atherosclerosis. Only two to three cloves of garlic a day may significantly decrease a person's risk of heart attack.

When it comes to antimicrobial activity, garlic kills microorganisms by direct contact. It may be mildly beneficial against some intestinal parasites, fungi, bacteria, and viruses. There are, however, no studies that show garlic is capable of killing organisms throughout the body.

Diets high in garlic have been shown to help prevent some types of cancer. People who eat garlic regularly have a decreased risk of developing cancers of the stomach, colon, and esophagus.[1] Garlic contains sulfur, selenium, and seventy-five different sulfur compounds. Studies have shown that people with diets high in the allium vegetables—such as garlic and onions—have a significantly decreased incidence of stomach cancer. Part of the cancer-preventive nature of garlic no doubt stems from its numerous antioxidant properties.

Eaten raw or taken as a syrup, garlic has been a popular remedy for colds, sore throats, and coughs. It has been prescribed by healers of various types as a diuretic and for intestinal disorders and rheumatism.

Many people avoid garlic because of its odor. The best way to reduce the aroma of garlic is to munch on a sprig or two of parsley—put that garnish on your restaurant plate to good use! To get the garlic odor off your hands, rub them with lemon juice and salt, then rinse.

Cooking does destroy or reduce the allicin in garlic, and it weakens some of garlic's other potent therapeutic benefits. Whether cooked, raw, or taken in extract form, however, garlic is one of the most potent natural healing foods known to man.

THE HEALTH BENEFITS OF ONIONS

Like its cousin, garlic, the onion has been regarded as a healing herb for thousands of years.

In ancient times, onions were considered a food that gave great energy and endurance. Slaves and laborers—many of them Israelites in Egypt— were fed diets rich in onions to keep the people strong for hard manual labor.

Onions have been used externally as an antiseptic and pain reliever, and taken internally as a tonic to ease intestinal gas pains and to alleviate the symptoms of hypertension, high blood sugar, and high cholesterol.

Bulgarians, who are known for their long life span, have traditionally attributed their longevity to a diet with high amounts of onions and yogurt.

Through the centuries, onions have especially been used to treat kidney and bladder problems. Modern herbalists believe onions to be a good expectorant and an excellent diuretic.

George Washington once was quoted as saying, "My own remedy is always to eat, just before I step into bed, a hot roasted onion, if I have a cold."

A great many research studies have demonstrated that onions raise HDL (good) cholesterol and lower LDL (bad) cholesterol. Onions slow blood clotting, regulate blood sugar, and may help prevent cancer.

A single tablespoon of cooked onions can help nullify some of the adverse effects of eating a meal that is high in fat.

Up to 150 different chemicals have been isolated in the onion. Many of these chemicals are still to be studied.

Raw onions seem to have more nutritional and therapeutic value than cooked onions. Cooking seems to reduce the onion's blood-cleansing and cholesterol-reducing powers, but these results still need to be tested further.

Of the 150 chemicals in onions, sulfur is a major one that induces enzyme systems in the liver that detoxify harmful compounds and help block tumor growth in animals.

Onions possess antibiotic properties that are effective against a variety of bacteria, fungi, and parasites. They also contain flavonoids, which are antioxidants that quench free radical reactions.

Just a half cup of raw onion contains the following:

Calories	27
Sodium	2 milligrams

Potassium	126 milligrams
Fiber	0.6 grams
Carbohydrates	5.9 grams

Onions are also high in vitamins, especially B_1 (thiamine), B_2 (riboflavin), and C.

LEEKS ARE SWEETER

A milder, sweeter version of the onion is the leek. In cooking, leeks are extremely versatile. Leeks have a more delicate flavor than either garlic or onions, and they form the base for many traditional dishes in ancient Israel. One such dish was a popular porridge made from the white bulb of the leek, rice (or other whole grain), crushed almonds, and honey as a sweetener.

Leeks were prescribed in quantity for infertile women. They were also prescribed by ancient people for obesity, kidney complaints, coughs, and intestinal disorders.

OTHER VEGETABLES
IMPORTANT FOR HEALTH

Let me remind you again of the Lord's provision as recorded in Genesis 1:29: "I have given you every herb that yields seed which is on the face of all the earth, and every tree whose fruit yields seed; to you it shall be for food." Put the emphasis on every herb and every tree whose fruit yields seed.

Many vegetables that are not commonly found in the Middle East are still valuable for our consumption today. In fact, the wider the variety of vegetables that we eat, the less likely we are to become bored with vegetables and the greater the nutritional benefit we will receive from them.

The U.S. Department of Agriculture recommends that a person eat from three to five servings of vegetables each day. I give a hearty second to that recommendation!

Many of the vegetables that have high amounts of phytonutrients—those nutrients that are most potent in protecting us from cancer and heart disease—are not mentioned in the Bible. They are not commonly available in Mediterranean nations, yet they are powerful allies for health.

CRUCIFEROUS VEGETABLES ARE DARK GREEN WONDERS

This large family of vegetables includes broccoli, cauliflower, Brussels sprouts, bok choy, collard greens, kale, mustard greens, watercress, turnip greens, radishes, rutabaga, horseradish, and cabbage. In fact, cruciferous vegetables are also commonly known as the cabbage-family vegetables. One of the main dietary recommendations of the American Cancer Society is that a person include cruciferous vegetables in the diet to help reduce the risk of cancer.

Cruciferous vegetables contain numerous anticancer compounds, including isothiocyanates, phenols, and sulfur-containing compounds such as sulphoraphanes and indoles. Broccoli is especially rich in isothiocyanates, sulphoraphanes, and indoles, such as indole-3-carbinol. These phytonutrients protect against cancer by stimulating the protective enzymes in the body—enzymes that are able to detoxify cancer-causing chemicals and rid them from the body. Indoles help prevent cancers that are dependent on hormones, such as breast cancer, by deactivating estrogens. Indole-3-carbinol is able to decrease estradiol, which is the most active form of estrogen, by converting the estradiol to estrone.

Having less estradiol and more estrone is associated with a decreased incidence of both breast and uterine cancer.[2]

Cabbage-family vegetables are also able to increase the body's production of one of the most important antioxidant enzymes in the body, glutathione peroxidase. They stimulate the liver to destroy cancer-causing agents. In addition, cruciferous vegetables contain folic acid, vitamin C, and beta carotene—all of which are important nutrients for good health. And finally, these vegetables provide a good source of nutritional fiber.

CAROTENOID VEGETABLES ARE HIGHLY COLORFUL

Carotenoids are found in yellow, orange, and red fruits and vegetables, as well as in dark green leafy vegetables. Carotenoids are actually red, yellow, and orange pigments—in dark leafy green vegetables, the color is concealed by the green of chlorophyll. There are more than six hundred different carotenoids. Beta carotene is perhaps the most familiar one.

Beta Carotene

Beta carotene is converted in the body to vitamin A, a strong stimulant for the immune system. Beta carotene seems especially capable of stimulating T-helper cells. It also functions as an antioxidant. Diets rich in foods that contain carotenoids are associated with a decreased risk of both cancer and heart disease.

Lycopene

Although beta carotene is the most widely known of the carotenoids, several other carotenoids have greater antioxidant activity. Lycopene is one of them.

Red-pigment foods containing lycopene include tomatoes, watermelons, pink grapefruit, apricots, and carrots.

Lycopene is an excellent antioxidant and also seems to have cancer-prevention properties. Studies involving prostate cancer have revealed these properties. Foods rich in lycopene also seem to have protective value against cancers of the colon, rectum, stomach, esophagus, and possibly other organs in the body.

Lutein

Foods high in lutein include spinach, collard greens, kale, romaine lettuce, and leeks. Eating foods high in lutein seems to help prevent cataracts and loss of vision.

Other Powerful Carotenoids

Other powerful carotenoids include alpha and gamma carotene, as well as zeaxanthin—all of which have greater antioxidant activity than beta carotene.

It is very unlikely that a person can get all of these powerful antioxidant carotenoids in a single vitamin tablet. The best approach for eating carotenoids is to eat plenty of carrots, tomatoes, squash, sweet potatoes, spinach, kale, and other dark green leafy vegetables. The best antioxidant protection is provided if a person eats a wide variety of carotenoid foods on a daily basis.

FOODS RICH IN CHLOROPHYLL

Another group of vegetables that contain powerful phytonutrients are those vegetables high in chlorophyll. Chlorophyll is responsible for the green pigment in plants. Generally speaking, the darker green the plant or vegetable, the more chlorophyll it contains.

Chlorophyll helps protect our DNA—our genetic blueprint—from various toxins. Two of these toxins are ones that have been linked to cancer—cigarette smoke and charred meat.

In addition to chlorophyll's anticancer properties, it has antioxidant effects.

Foods high in chlorophyll include spinach, kale, collard greens, beet tops, and parsley.

If you eat charcoal-grilled or fried foods, I strongly suggest you consume one of these high chlorophyll foods to block any cancer-causing chemicals that are produced as a result of frying or charcoal grilling.

COMBINING VEGETABLES AND GRAINS

Most vegetables and grains are incomplete proteins, which means they do not have all the essential amino acids. Soy is the exception. (Dairy products, meat, and eggs contain all the food-supplied amino acids required by the human body.)

To come up with a complete protein, a person needs to eat a mixture of the seeds, beans, nuts, and grains that have incomplete protein. For example, if you combine beans with brown rice, you have a complete protein. If you combine beans with nuts and seeds, you have a complete protein.

What do I mean by a complete protein? There are eight essential amino acids—essential meaning that these amino acids cannot be produced in the body and must be provided by our food. In other words, it is "essential" for us to get these amino acids from the food we eat.

Complete proteins such as meat, dairy, eggs, and soy have all eight essential amino acids. Grains tend to be low in the amino acid lysine. However, beans and legumes have high amounts of lysine. Beans have low amounts of methionine and cysteine—grains have a higher content of these two amino acids. When a person eats beans and grains together, all of the essential amino acids are provided. The protein in combination is "complete."

Think about how many Mexican food dishes are accompanied by rice and beans. There's a good nutritional reason for this. Unfortunately, the beans served in most Mexican restaurants are refried, with large amounts of fat, and the rice is white, stripped of all bran and germ. In other words, the protein may be complete, but the fat content and low nutritional value of the rice make the foods far less acceptable nutritionally. A hearty meal of whole grains and beans, however, is a good high-protein meal. No meat or animal products are even required!

The Bible gives an excellent example of this "combining" effect of protein. When the Babylonians captured the Israelites, they took a number of the youth to Babylon. These youth were of noble descent, "young men in whom there was no blemish, but good-looking, gifted in all wisdom, possessing knowledge and quick to understand, who had ability to serve in the king's palace, and whom they might teach the language and literature of the Chaldeans" (Dan. 1:4).

Daniel was among those taken into exile, along with his friends Hananiah, Mishael, and Azariah. (Daniel's name was changed in Babylon to Belteshazzar, and the other three were given the Babylonian names of Shadrach, Meshach, and Abed-Nego.) These four young men were put into language and literature classes and were given a portion of the king's own dietary fare. The Bible says they were given wine to drink and delicacies from the king's table.

But Daniel and his three friends refused to eat this food. The foods were likely those forbidden by the Law of Moses. It is also highly likely that the meat they were served had been sacrificed to false gods, since that was customary in Babylon.

Daniel made it known to the eunuch in charge of their care that he would not eat the king's food. He said to the eunuch, "Please test your servants for ten days, and let them give us vegetables to eat and water to drink. Then let our countenances be examined before you, and the countenances of the young men who eat the portion of the king's delicacies; and as you see fit, so deal with your servants." The eunuch agreed (Dan. 1:12–14).

At the end of the ten days, their appearances appeared fairer and "fatter in flesh" than those who had been eating the king's delicacies. They continued to eat vegetables and water for the next three years.

The actual word for their food is *pulse*, which is a mixture of vegetables and grains such as wheat, barley, rye, peas, beans, and lentils. Again, these grains and beans form a complete protein when eaten together, and if the substances included sprouted grains and beans, the foods would have been even higher in nutritional content.

At the end of the three years, the king found that these four young men were "ten times better than all the magicians and astrologers who were in his realm" in matters of "wisdom and understanding" (Dan. 1:20). Nothing about their diet had diminished their brain capacity in the least!

I have no doubt at all that Jesus ate a diversity of garlic, onions, vegetables, beans, and lentils. He also ate incomplete proteins in combinations that resulted in complete protein supplied to His body.

VEGETABLES AS A VALUABLE SOURCE OF FIBER

A number of scientific studies have shown that diets rich in fruits and vegetables decrease a person's risk of developing both cancer and heart disease. Part of the reason for this is the high-fiber content of fruits and vegetables that are eaten in the whole, fresh form.

Fiber helps lower cholesterol levels, stabilizes blood sugar, slows digestion, and has been shown to help prevent hemorrhoids, irritable bowel syndrome, varicose veins, constipation, obesity, and even colon cancer. Fiber in the lower intestinal tract helps bind heavy metals, toxins, and chemicals and remove them from the body before they can be absorbed and cause damage to cells and tissues. When carcinogens and toxins are removed from the colon, a person has much less likelihood of developing colon cancer.

Several decades ago the renowned British physician Dr. Dennis Burkitt spent time working as a surgeon in Africa. He noticed that he rarely had to operate on Africans who consumed a traditional high-fiber African diet. In comparison, he frequently had to perform surgery on the British people who had colonized the area. He further noted that the British tended to eat a diet consisting primarily of refined foods.

Burkitt undertook a study involving the bowel movements and stools of rural Africans and the British naval officers in his practice.

The rural Africans ate a diet that usually included more than one hundred grams of fiber a day. The British naval officers ate a diet rich in meat, white flour, and refined sugar.

The Africans had large stools that tended to pass effortlessly from their bodies, with the average time span from eating to elimination being 18 to 36 hours. In comparison, the British had small, compact stools that tended to pass with difficulty—the time span from ingestion to elimination was 72 to 100 hours.

The British naval officers had much higher instances of hemorrhoids, anal fissures, varicose veins, diverticulitis, diverticulosis, thrombophlebitis, gallbladder disease, appendicitis, hiatal hernias, irritable bowel syndrome, obesity, high cholesterol, coronary artery disease, high blood pressure, diabetes, hypoglycemia, colon polyps, and colon and rectal cancers.

The rural Africans experienced these diseases and conditions only when they converted to a British diet rich in meat, white flour, and refined sugar—which tended to happen as the Africans attended school in England. Dr. Burkitt concluded that when fiber is removed from the diet, many of the diseases that plague modern civilization occur.[3]

Americans consume only about ten grams of fiber a day, and we should be consuming approximately twenty-five to thirty-five grams of fiber a day.

Soluble fibers are broken down by intestinal microorganisms and provide the fuel for maintaining a healthy lining of the intestinal tract. Soluble fiber also binds bile salts in the intestines, which helps to lower cholesterol and prevent gallbladder disease.

Increased fiber is associated with decreased hunger and, thus, can be a good means for aiding weight loss.

Soluble or Insoluble

One of the main ways to classify fiber is according to its solubility in water.

Insoluble fibers are not water soluble, and these include lignin and cellulose. Bran is the most common source of fiber—and wheat bran is the most common source of bran. This type of fiber increases the weight of the stool as well as the frequency of bowel movements, thus preventing constipation, hemorrhoids, and other intestinal disorders. Good sources of insoluble fiber include the skins of vegetables and fruits, whole grains, dried beans, bulgur wheat, and high-fiber cereals.

Good sources of soluble fiber are fruits, garbanzo beans, lentils, navy beans, carrots, barley, oats, and rice.

There are seven main types of fiber:

1. *Cellulose*. Cellulose is the indigestible form of fiber found in the outer layers of fruits and vegetables. Wheat bran is rich in cellulose and is

relatively insoluble in water. This type of fiber is excellent for treating constipation, hemorrhoids, and varicose veins.

2. *Hemicellulose*. Hemicellulose is an indigestible complex carbohydrate that absorbs water. It is found in plant cell walls, whole-grain cereals, apples, beans, and green leafy vegetables.

3. *Pectin*. Pectin, the substance that holds plant tissue together, is found in all plant cell walls as well as the outer skin and rind of fruits and vegetables. Pectin is found in apples, carrots, citrus fruits, peas, apple peels, and other peelings of fruits and vegetables.

4. *Gum*. This type of fiber is similar to hemicellulose but is found on the inner layer or the endosperm layer of nuts, seeds, legumes, and grains.

5. *Mucilage*. This type of fiber is the same as the gums. Guar gum, psyllium husk, and glucomannan are examples of mucilages.

6. *Lignin*. This form of fiber is excellent for lowering cholesterol and helping to prevent gallstones. Lignins have anticancer, antifungal, antibacterial, and antiviral activity. They are believed to help protect against breast cancer. Flaxseed is the most abundant source of lignins, but whole-grain legumes and seeds also are good sources of lignins.

7. *Algal polysaccharide*. This last major type of fiber is a product of seaweed.

Add Fiber Slowly

It is important for a person who is low in fiber consumption to increase fiber slowly to avoid developing excessive bloating, gas, and cramps. It may take a month or longer to introduce sufficient high-fiber foods into one's diet. Start by choosing whole-grain bread over white bread, choose whole fruits over juices, and choose a baked potato, including the skin, over potato chips or mashed potatoes. Gradually introduce more beans and whole grains into the diet.

Another way to increase fiber in one's diet is to take a fiber supplement, such as psyllium, rice bran, oat bran, or wheat bran. Always take in sufficient water when increasing your intake of fiber. Drink a minimum of two quarts of water a day—or one ounce of water for every two pounds of body weight. Also be careful not to eat wheat bran with vitamins since the phytic acid in wheat bran can bind minerals such as magnesium, zinc, and iron. If you are choosing a fiber supplement, take it at a different time than you take your vitamin and mineral supplements.

The best way to obtain all the major types of fiber in one's diet is to consume a diet rich in whole grains, beans, and fresh whole fruits and vegetables.

ENHANCING THE TASTE OF VEGETABLES

I recently heard about a woman who went to a restaurant on the central coast of California and ordered a green salad. The waiter forgot to bring her dressing on the side, so she began to pick out various greens with her fingers and nibble them. She was amazed at their taste and exclaimed to her friends, "I'm fifty-two years old, and this is the first time I've tasted lettuce!"

The produce at that particular restaurant was very fresh—the lettuce and other greens had been picked that very morning from farms just about twenty miles away. All her life this woman had eaten produce that was not locally grown, and that had been smothered in heavy salad dressings. She was amazed at the taste of greens she thought she knew well.

Whenever possible, I recommend that a person eat locally grown, organic produce. A great family activity is a weekly trip to the nearest farmer's market to select fruits and vegetables that may still have some dirt clinging to them, but are unlikely to have pesticides or waxes added to them.

One of the things that many people discover when they begin to eat the way Jesus ate is that they enjoy the taste of fresh food as never before. The truth is, many people in our nation have grown accustomed to eating foods that are laden with salt, sugar, additives, hydrogenated fats, and other items used in the processing of food. As a nation, we seem to have forgotten what whole, fresh food tastes like.

JUST ADD SALT AND PEPPER?

One of the most common practices in cooking is to add salt and pepper to virtually every dish. While salt and pepper may be good additives for some foods, I recommend that a person limit his or her salt intake.

Sugar addiction has been recognized for decades, but salt addiction is a relatively new area of study. Some people seem to crave salty foods, and food manufacturers are quick to capitalize on that fact.

Salt is composed of sodium and chloride. Sodium is a major culprit related to ill health. Most Americans ingest twice as much sodium as potassium. But for optimum health, a potassium to sodium ratio of 5:1 or greater is recommended. That means, five times as much potassium should be consumed as sodium. The amount of sodium required to maintain a good sodium-potassium equilibrium for most adults is less than 200 milligrams of salt a day—that is equal to about a tenth of a teaspoon of salt a day. A typical American adult consumes 6 to 25 grams of salt a day, with a mean of about 10 grams a day. That is twenty times more than the correct amount!

I routinely encounter patients who tell me, "I never salt my food." What they mean is that they rarely use a salt shaker at a table. They falsely believe that their salt intake is low, even though processed foods make up a large part of their diet. The sad fact is that processed foods are very high in sodium content. Check the label the next time you pick up a can of soup or vegetables.

Those who crave salt are often people who feel fatigued and exhausted. These people tend to have sluggish adrenal function.

Approximately one out of four adult Americans suffers from hypertension, or high blood pressure, and excessive sodium intake has been linked.

The best ways to change this ratio and to increase potassium intake are to eat more fresh fruits and vegetables, which have a higher concentration of potassium than sodium; to decrease dramatically the intake of processed and fast foods; and to stop using a salt shaker. If you love the taste of salt, use a salt substitute such as NoSalt or Nu-Salt. If you must use salt, choose Celtic salt available in most health food stores.

SPICES AND HERBS USED IN JESUS' TIME

People in Bible times used a wide variety of herbs and spices, not only for their ability to flavor food but also for their medicinal purposes. Only a few of these noted here are mentioned in the Bible.

Coriander

Manna looked like coriander seeds to the Israelites. Coriander is better known to many people today as cilantro. It has been called "the healer from heaven."

Coriander is an annual plant of the parsley or carrot family. The fruit of the plant consists of grayish-white globular seeds, which have a pleasant, aromatic oil. Coriander has been used to flavor pastries, meats, candies, salads, curries, soups, and even wine.

Coriander has been used for centuries to treat minor stomach ailments, including indigestion, flatulence, and diarrhea. It has also been applied topically to ease muscle and joint pain.

A good yogurt-based condiment for use with grilled chicken, lamb, or fish can be made by adding a clove of garlic, one tablespoon of vinegar, a half teaspoon of salt, and a half teaspoon of cumin to a cup of chopped coriander leaves and eight ounces of yogurt. Blend this, and chill it well before serving.

Hyssop

Many Bible scholars believe that hyssop was a type of marjoram, part of the mint family. Hyssop grew abundantly in Israel and the Sinai Peninsula during Bible times, and it still is used extensively in the Middle East for flavoring and in medicinal teas.

Hyssop is known to help prevent blood from coagulating. It is an age-old decongestant. It has also been shown in modern experiments to halt the growth of the herpes simplex virus, which causes cold sores and genital herpes. Dr. James Balch states that hyssop promotes the expulsion of mucus from the respiratory tract, relieves congestion, regulates blood pressure, and dispels gas.

Mint

Although the taste of mint is very pleasant to most people, mint is listed among the herbs that many Bible scholars believe were "bitter herbs" in Exodus 12:8 and Numbers 9:11. Other bitter herbs are believed to be the leaves of endive, chicory, lettuce, watercress, sorrel, and dandelion—all of which were eaten as something of a "salad" in Bible times. The two main species of mint that grow throughout the Middle East are peppermint and spearmint.

The Romans and Greeks used mint to keep milk from spoiling. They routinely offered mint after meals as a digestive aid. Modern herbalists recommend peppermint for menstrual cramps, morning sickness, colds, flu, motion sickness, heartburn, fever, headache, and insomnia.

Mint is also an antispasmodic. Mint soothes the muscles of the digestive tract and uterus. It has been shown to be good for nausea, as well as to stimulate menstruation. Women who have a history of miscarriages should avoid peppermint as a treatment for morning sickness.

Parsley

The Bible identifies a group of plants as "scented herbs" (Song 5:13). Parsley is thought to have been one of these herbs. It grows profusely in Israel. It is one of the first herbs to appear in the spring, which is perhaps why it is part of most traditional Passover meals.

Parsley is a rich source of vitamins A and C. Two of the chemicals in parsley, apiol and myristicin, act as a mild laxative and a strong diuretic. Its diuretic action may help control high blood pressure. In Germany, parsley tea is often prescribed for that purpose.

Scientific research has shown that parsley blocks the formation of histamines, the chemical that triggers allergy attacks. It may help those who suffer from hay fever or have an outbreak of hives. Dr. James Balch states parsley relieves gas, stimulates normal activity of the digestive system, and freshens breath. It also helps bladder, kidney, liver, lung, stomach, and thyroid function. It is good for bed-wetting, hypertension, edema, bad breath, gas, and kidney disease.

Other Herbs

Herbs such as dill, cumin, turmeric, cinnamon, saffron, and mustard are all common spices in Middle Eastern cooking. Although they are not mentioned in the Bible, they are great flavor enhancers. I encourage you to experiment with them.

WHAT WOULD JESUS EAT?

Jesus ate a diet loaded with vegetables, especially garlic, onions, leeks, beans, and lentils—these vegetables were often a main dish and were routinely enhanced with herbs and spices common to Israel.

We can eat as Jesus ate by adding more vegetables to our diet, and by eating these fresh, whole vegetables raw, lightly steamed or lightly fried in olive oil.

CHAPTER SEVEN

THE FATS THAT
JESUS ATE

THE FATS WE TEND TO EAT IN AMERICA TODAY ARE not the same fats that Jesus ate. Unfortunately, we suffer as a result.

Americans as a whole are eating way too many saturated fats, hydrogenated fats, partially hydrogenated fats, and refined, highly processed polyunsaturated fats. They are also consuming too many fried foods.

Saturated fats are primarily found in dairy products, meats, lard, many fried foods, and eggs. Whole milk, ice cream, creamers, visible and marbled fats in hamburger meat and steaks, and chicken skins are special culprits in this category.

Hydrogenated fats are found primarily in margarine, shortening, and peanut butters.

Partially hydrogenated fats are routinely added to processed foods to increase flavor and "mouth texture." These fats are found in chips, crackers, pizza, salad dressing, mayonnaise, frozen dinners, cookies, cakes, snack foods, and pies.

Polyunsaturated fats actually come from the unsaturated fatty acids of vegetables, grains, nuts, and seeds. However, the majority of these fats available to the American consumer are found in the form of highly processed and refined oils—soybean oil, safflower oil, sunflower oil, corn oil, and cottonseed oil. The problem here is not only the source of the fat, but especially the refining process that produces lipid peroxides, which create free radicals that in turn cause great damage to the body at the cellular level.

Furthermore, polyunsaturated fats, when exposed to light, heat, and air, become rancid rather quickly. Even partial rancidity—the kind we cannot yet smell or taste—is damaging to our health.

Probably the most dangerous of the fats are the hydrogenated fats, which include margarine, most processed peanut butter, and shortening. These fats are made by heating polyunsaturated oils to a very high temperature and then bubbling hydrogen gas through the oil until it becomes hardened. The manufacturer's goal is to stabilize the oil so that it has a longer shelf life. However, the creation of hydrogenated fats is the result.

The health damage is caused not only by the release of free radicals that damages cells in the body, but also by an interference with the body's ability to use the essential fatty acids. When the ability to use fatty acids is diminished, cholesterol levels may rise, increasing a person's risk of heart attack and cardiovascular disease.

The standard American diet provides approximately 37 percent of its total calories from fat.[1] The majority of this fat is in the form of polyunsaturated and saturated fats.

Our goal when it comes to fat consumption should be twofold: first, to decrease the percentage of our diet from fat, and second, to make sure that nearly all of our fat-related calories come from natural foods and monounsaturated oils, such as olive oil.

THE HARMFUL EFFECTS FROM PROCESSING OIL

Just as most people do not understand how their white flour is processed, they do not usually understand how the oil they use is processed either.

Most processed oil comes from natural seeds such as sunflower seeds. These seeds are heated to high temperatures of approximately 250 degrees Fahrenheit, and then the seed is pressed to expel the oil. The oil in this process is unavoidably subjected to heat and pressure, which increase the rancidity of the oil.

Then, solvents—similar to gasoline—are added to the oil to dissolve the oil out of the grain. The oil is then heated to more than 300 degrees to evaporate the solvent.

In the next step, the oil is degummed, a process that removes most of the nutrients—including minerals such as calcium, magnesium, iron, and copper, as well as chlorophyll, phospholipids, and lecithin.

By this time the oil has a yellowish tinge, so it is bleached at high temperatures, which cause more rancidity and more lipid peroxides to form. The damaged oil is then deodorized at temperatures of more than 500 degrees for thirty minutes to an hour.

The end result is an odorless, clear oil that appears sterile and pure, but is in fact full of toxic lipid peroxides that can cause significant free-radical reactions leading to cardiovascular disease and cancer.

THE HEALTHFUL ALTERNATIVE: OLIVE OIL

When the Israelites were still wandering in the wilderness, they received a promise from God that they would be led to a "land of olive oil" (Deut. 8:8). Indeed, they were.

The olive tree is one of the longest living trees—many live longer than a thousand years, and some trees alive in Israel today are estimated to have been alive two thousand years ago when Jesus walked the earth. A few of these ancient olive trees are in the area of the Garden of Gethsemane.

Not only are olive trees long lived, but they are also among the most resilient of trees. Through the ages, wars have ravaged the land of Israel, and many of the olive orchards have been cut down. The olive tree, however, seems to have a unique ability to grow back even when it appears to be dead.

Bread made during the time of Jesus was a "flat bread" similar to pita bread, and it was made using olive oil. The best breads were made with the purest flour and the purest olive oil, and these were brought to the temple of Jerusalem as an offering.

In 1 Kings 17, we find the story of Elijah and the widow of Zarephath. Elijah was directed to Zarephath at the height of a great famine. There he encountered a single mother, a widow, who was gathering sticks in anticipation of building a small fire to cook the last of her meal and oil as a little cake for herself and her son. Elijah met her and asked her to bring him some water and to give him a morsel of bread. She replied that all she had was a handful of meal in a barrel and a little oil in a jar.

Three handfuls of meal were usually required to make a loaf of flat bread—in other words, she had only the ingredients for about a third of a loaf of bread.

Elijah prophesied to her:

> Do not fear . . . make me a small cake from it first, and bring it to me; and afterward make some for yourself and your son. For thus says the LORD God of Israel: "The bin of flour shall not be used up, nor shall the jar of oil run dry, until the day the LORD sends rain on the earth." (1 Kings 17:13–14)

The woman did as Elijah requested, and we read later in this chapter that her barrel of meal did not run out for nearly three years, and neither did the jar of oil.

For the vast majority of history, olives have been abundant in the land of Israel. In 1 Kings 5:11 we read that King Solomon gave Hiram, the king of Tyre, an annual gift in exchange for the cedars of Lebanon that were shipped from Tyre for the building of the temple. This gift from Solomon included "twenty thousand measures of wheat as food for his household, and twenty measures of pressed oil." Twenty measures of pressed oil were more than one hundred thousand gallons of olive oil!

The Pressing of Olives

The olive tree was first cultivated in the Mediterranean countries more than six thousand years ago. Many believe it was first cultivated in Greece. Today, Spain and Italy produce more than 50 percent of the world's olives and olive oil. California is the leading state in olive production in the United States.

During the days of Jesus, olives were eaten both raw and cooked, but most olives were pressed into oil.

On the night before His crucifixion, Jesus went to the Garden of Gethsemane to pray. This garden was located on the lower hillside of the Mount of Olives—aptly named for its olive groves. Olive trees were grown there so the oil might be harvested and taken directly across the deep valley to the temple. These trees produced the oil that burned in the large lamp stands of the temple, as well as the oil used for bread and meal sacrifices and for the making of the showbread. The groves were within a Sabbath day's journey of the temple, which allowed the oil to be carried from olive presses to the temple even on a Sabbath should the temple run short.

The word Gethsemane is derived from the word in Hebrew that literally means "oil press." The Garden of Gethsemane was, therefore, the garden with the olive press.

Olive oil was extracted from olives using large wooden presses. In Old Testament times, some olive oil was extracted by the treading of olives by feet. In Micah 6:15 we read: "You shall tread the olives, but not anoint yourselves with oil." Some olive oil was also extracted by pressing the fruit with a round millstone.

Not only was olive oil used for cooking, but it was also used as an ointment for making medicines, as part of cosmetics, and as a component of soap. Even today, castile soap is made of pure olive oil.

Not only were the temple lamps filled with olive oil, but also the lamps of the people's homes. Jesus told a parable about ten virgins who took their lamps and went out to meet the bridegroom, and only five of them had sufficient oil to light their way during the bridal procession (See Matt. 25:1–13). These lamps would have burned olive oil.

Symbolically, olive oil was used for anointing. Prophets were anointed with oil when they assumed their duties (See 1 Kings 19:16). Priests were anointed with oil (Lev. 8:12), and kings were anointed with oil by either a prophet or a priest (1 Sam. 16:13). Throughout the Scriptures, the anointing by olive oil typically symbolized the impartation of the Holy Spirit.

It was a common practice of hospitality to provide oil for a guest so he might anoint his own hair, face, and hands with it—something of a hair and skin dressing prior to the partaking of a meal. The washing of feet and hands and the anointing of oil on hair and skin signaled the beginning of a proper meal. Psalm 23:5 says,

> You prepare a table before me in the presence of my enemies;
> You anoint my head with oil;
> My cup runs over.

The use of oil in this manner at the start of a meal signaled that the meal was one partaken of by all parties in the presence of God's Spirit— an atmosphere of congeniality, faith, and love was expected.

The practice of anointing with oil was also associated with healing, a practice that continues in the church today. In James 5:14 we read, "Is anyone among you sick? Let him call for the elders of the church, and let them pray over him, anointing him with oil in the name of the Lord."

THE USE OF OLIVE OIL IN COOKING

From ancient times olive oil was used in the making of bread and as an ingredient in many other dishes. Olive oil was also used as the butter for bread. Even today, olive oil to which cracked pepper or other spices and herbs have been added is called "Italian butter"—morsels of bread are dipped into the oil at the time of eating. (By the way, Italians consume one hundred times more olive oil than Americans consume).[2]

DIFFERENCES IN OLIVE OILS

All olive oil is not equal. It comes in different grades depending on the pressing from which the oil is derived. In the pressing of olives, whole, undamaged olives are pressed mechanically several times without heat. In fact, the temperature of olive oil extraction ranges from 58 to 110 degrees Fahrenheit. Extra virgin olive oil is oil from the first pressing of olives; the oil is extracted, filtered, and undergoes no further refining. It is the highest quality oil. Very strict guidelines exist for a product to be named "extra virgin." Virgin olive oil is from the end of the first pressing or the second pressing.

For maximum health benefits, olive oil that is consumed should be extra virgin or virgin olive oil. If a bottle of olive oil is not labeled as "extra virgin" or "virgin," then the oil has been refined in some way. If olives have been damaged and started to spoil, the olive oil is of lesser quality and must be refined. The same for pressings of the fruit that occur after the second pressing. In the refining process, olive oil is degummed, refined, bleached, and deodorized. It is heated above 300 degrees Fahrenheit, which chemically changes the oil and causes it to lose many of its health effects.[3]

When olive oil was used as an offering, it was oil from the first crush of the purest and finest olives, brought to the temple in sealed jars.[4]

Just one tablespoon of olive oil has the following:

Calories	119
Vitamin E	3–30 mg
Monounsaturated fatty acids (oleic)	56–83%
Polyunsaturated unfatty acids (linoleic)	3.5–20%
Saturated fatty acids	8.0–23.5%

Olive oil is composed primarily of monounsaturated fat, specifically oleic acid, which makes up about 75 percent of the fat in olive oil. Oleic acid has been shown to lower cholesterol levels.

Olive oil also contains a saturated fat called palmitic acid, which comprises about 10 percent of olive oil and the polyunsaturated fat, linoleic acid, which also averages 10 percent. Several other saturated fatty acids, as well as another monounsaturated fatty acid, comprise the fat content of the remaining 15 percent.

The monounsaturated fats as well as the low amount of saturated fat in olive oil make the oil very stable, which gives it a long shelf life. Olive oil does not require refrigeration, unlike polyunsaturated fats that readily become rancid.

Many people assume that when they read the term *fatty acids*, they are reading about something to be avoided, but the exact opposite is true. As we discussed in the chapter on fish, we need essential fatty acids for health! The average person has approximately sixty to one hundred trillion cells in the body, and every one of those cells is surrounded by a fatty cell membrane. It is the cell membrane that allows nutrients to enter the cell and that allows waste to be expelled from the cell. In the brain, cell membranes allow for the quick and efficient flow of electrical impulses, which is directly related to clear thinking and memory. The essential fatty acids help maintain membrane development and improve cell membrane function. Extra virgin olive oil is a great aid to cell membrane development and health.

Olive oil has been shown to help decrease LDL (bad) cholesterol levels and increase HDL (good) cholesterol levels. In contrast, polyunsaturated fats such as sunflower, safflower, corn, and soybean oil lower good cholesterol and lower bad cholesterol. However, they also caused an increase in oxidation of LDL cholesterol. Dr. Daniel Steinberg at the University of California actually found that olive oil blocks the oxidation of LDL cholesterol. He gave one group of volunteers approximately 40 percent of their calories from fat in monounsaturated fats—approximately three tablespoons of olive oil a day. The other group received safflower oil, a polyunsaturated fat. Bad cholesterol was examined in both groups at a later date, and the group that had consumed olive oil was found to have half the oxidation of their LDL cholesterol. Oxidized cholesterol is much more likely to form plaque and thus clog arteries. Anything a person can do to keep LDL cholesterol from oxidizing is valuable![5]

Another significant landmark study in this area was conducted in the 1950s by Dr. Keyes and his colleagues. They followed twelve thousand middle-aged men in seven different countries for thirty years. The mortality rates for coronary heart disease were significantly lower for Greek men, when compared to Northern European, Japanese, and American groups.[6]

The island of Crete has one of the lowest incidences of heart disease and cancer. Approximately 45 percent of the calories in the people's diet comes from fat, and about 33 percent of these calories are from olive oil. Residents of Crete consume more olive oil per person than any other nation. They sometimes drink olive oil by the glass! In a fifteen-year period, 38 out of 10,000 Cretans died of heart disease, as compared to 773 out of 10,000 Americans. In other words, the United States had twenty times as much heart disease as Crete.

Most other Mediterranean nations also have low rates of heart disease, even though the people in these nations eat more fat than Americans. The difference is that 75 percent of their fat calories come from monounsaturated fats (olive oil). In Italy, physicians usually recommend olive oil to patients after they have had heart attacks. One of the reasons for this is the beneficial properties of olive oil on platelet function. Olive oil helps decrease the stickiness of platelets, thus helping prevent coronary thrombosis and blood clots.[7]

Olive oil also functions in the body to stimulate the gallbladder to contract. This helps to eliminate biliary sludge and even small gallstones. You should consult your physician, however, before consuming olive oil for this purpose.

Olive oil helps relieve constipation since it functions as a mild, natural laxative. One to two tablespoons at bedtime are usually recommended as a dose to help relieve constipation.

Olive oil also has other nutritional components—generally known as minor components nutritionally. These include antioxidants such as vitamin E, beta carotene, lecithin, chlorophyll, and squalenes, which help deliver oxygen to tissue. It also contains phytosterols, which help lower cholesterol levels, as well as polyphenols, which have antioxidant properties and immune-enhancing properties. Many other phytonutrients are found in olives, all of which have health-promoting effects.

Benefit from Roots and Leaves

Olive leaf extract—which is obtained not from the olives but from olive leaves—is rich in phytochemicals, the most effective of which is oleuropein. According to James Balch, M.D., olive leaf extract has been shown to be effective against virtually all viruses and bacteria on which it has been tested. It has been shown useful in treating sore throat, sinusitis, skin diseases, as well as fungal and bacterial infections. It may also prove helpful for chronic fatigue syndrome, inflammatory arthritis, psoriasis, as well as diarrheal disease.[8]

Roots of olive trees were used in construction. Growing up in a carpenter's home, Jesus was likely very familiar with the use of olive wood in the construction of cabinets, doors, and pieces of furniture. In 1 Kings 6 we read that King Solomon ordered that the cherubim of the temple, the inner and outer doors, and the posts of the sanctuary all be made of olive wood.[9]

INCORPORATING OLIVE OIL INTO THE DIET

One of the best ways to incorporate extra virgin olive oil into the diet is to use it on salads as a dressing. Combine it with balsamic or apple cider vinegar. (A recipe is found in the last chapter of this book.)

It is also a good idea to use olive oil instead of butter or polyunsaturated fats in cooking.

As you make a change to olive oil, do so gradually. (As noted, olive oil does have a laxative effect.)

WHAT WOULD JESUS EAT?

Jesus very likely consumed extra virgin olive oil on a daily basis.

We can follow His example by using olive oil instead of butter, other oils, and salad dressing. Olive oil is the best choice for both cooking and eating!

CHAPTER EIGHT

THE BEVERAGES THAT JESUS DRANK

NOT TOO LONG AGO, A FRIEND OF MINE ASKED A waitress what in her experience she had found to be the most commonly ordered beverage. She indicated that the most popular order was for soft drinks. The second most popular beverage was "water with lemon." I give a big round of applause to the number two choice!

One beverage we know with certainty that Jesus drank was water. One of the most famous stories of Jesus in the New Testament dealt with His drinking water. In John 4 we read that Jesus was on his way to Galilee from Jerusalem, and as He passed through Samaria, He and His disciples were tired from their journey and sat by a well. The disciples went on into the town of Sychar to buy food, and Jesus remained at the well. A woman of Samaria came to draw water, and Jesus said to her, "Give Me a drink."

The woman was surprised that Jesus asked her to draw water for Him since Jews and Samaritans had little to do with one another, but she complied. Jesus said to her, "If you knew the gift of God, and who it is who says to you, 'Give Me a drink,' you would have asked Him, and He would have given you living water" (John 4:10). He was referring to the gift of eternal life and the indwelling presence of God's Spirit.

Women in the time of Jesus were responsible for supplying their homes with water. They were trained from early childhood to bring water from wells or springs, usually in the late afternoon or evening. A woman generally carried her own pitcher to the well, drew water, and then carried the water home either on her head or on her shoulder. Sometimes several trips to the well were necessary to provide an adequate amount of water for the household. In some cases, a woman also needed to bring her own bucket and rope for drawing water. The well at Sychar apparently did not have a bucket and rope, and that is why He asked the woman to draw water for Him because she said to Him, "You have nothing to draw with, and the well is deep. Where then do You get that living water?" (John 4:11).

Water has always been a precious commodity in Israel. Without it, the people die. Wells were dug deep, and well guarded. The famous well where Jesus met this Samaritan woman was a well the people believed had been dug in the time of Jacob and given to his son Joseph. It still exists today.

As the Israelites wandered in the wilderness of the Sinai Peninsula, they had a desperate need for water on two occasions. In both cases, water was supplied to them supernaturally. In Exodus 17:6, we read how the Lord commanded Moses to strike a rock, and when he did, water gushed forth. Again in Numbers 20:8, God instructed Moses to take his rod and speak to a rock for it to give water. The Israelites must have longed for the promised land that was in their future—a land God had told them would be a "good land, a land of brooks of water, of fountains and springs, that flow out of valleys and hills" (Deut. 8:7).

THE MOST IMPORTANT NUTRIENT FOR THE BODY

Water is the most important nutrient for the human body. Indeed, the human body consists primarily of water—approximately two-thirds of a person's body weight is water.

The average person who is conscious and moving can live for approximately forty days without food, but only about three to five days without water. Water is necessary for nearly every bodily function, including circulation, digestion, absorption, and excretion. Water is vital for carrying nutrients to all cells of the body. Every cell in the body produces metabolic waste products of some form—commonly lactic acid, urea, and uric acid. An adequate water intake is essential to remove these waste products from the body via the bloodstream and excretory organs.

The major constituent of all the fluids in the body is water: saliva, gastric juice, bile, pancreatic juices, intestinal secretions, and blood. The synovial fluid, which lubricates the joints, is composed primarily of water. Patients with joint pain and arthritis definitely need an extra intake of water to provide lubrication for their joints.

Many individuals develop degenerative disc disease in their necks and backs as they age. This is usually caused by discs simply wearing out owing to inadequate fluid within the disc. The disc is composed of a fibrous material called the annulus fibrosus, and it is filled with a jellyike substance called *nucleus pulposus*. This jellylike material is composed primarily of water. When the discs become dehydrated, they are more prone to degenerate and eventually herniate, and thus many develop degenerative disc disease and arthritis. A person who continues to drive a car with a nearly flat tire will eventually find that the tire wears out or "blows." A similar process occurs with the discs of the back—if they are "flat" owing to too little fluid, they eventually degenerate or herniate.

Joints are covered by cartilage, which is approximately five times slicker than ice and composed of 80 percent water. If cartilage becomes dehydrated and the synovial fluid is insufficient, increased friction results, causing damage to the cartilage, and eventually leading to arthritis.

Adequate intake of water is also vital for lung function. Lung tissue that is thoroughly moist is capable of greater oxygen intake and also greater excretion of carbon dioxide.

Adequate water intake is necessary to improve blood pressure in persons with hypertension, high cholesterol levels, obesity, diabetes, asthma, gastrointestinal problems, hiatal hernias, headaches, angina, allergies, and constipation. Adequate water intake also helps prevent kidney stones and can slow the aging process. The latter is accomplished primarily because adequate water keeps the cells nourished by carrying nutrients to the cells and removing cellular waste products.

Finally, those who take in adequate amounts of water generally find they have increased energy because they are healthier at the cellular level.

HOW MUCH WATER SHOULD WE DRINK?

In my medical practice, the first advice I give patients with any of the above-mentioned diseases is to increase their water intake to at least two to three quarts of filtered water a day. I have found among my patients that adequate water intake has been directly related to the elimination of headaches, improved blood pressure, improved arthritis pain, back pain, and neck pain, and even at times, the complete elimination of these conditions. In general, I find that patients with all chronic illnesses have fewer symptoms and better overall health as they increase their water intake.

A person should drink at least two to three quarts of filtered or distilled water a day. A more precise calculation is this:

Write down your body weight in pounds.

Divide this number by 2.

Drink that many ounces of water a day. Remember that eight ounces of water is one cup, and there are four cups in a quart.

For example, if a person weighs two hundred pounds, then half of that is one hundred. One hundred ounces is equal to twelve and a half cups of water, or three quarts plus one-half cup.

I recommend that a person drink eight to sixteen ounces of water upon awakening, and then drink at least a cup of water, or two, thirty minutes prior to each meal and again two hours after a meal. Keep the flow of water running through your body all day.

At mealtimes, limit your consumption of fluids to only four to eight ounces. The optimum water intake for digestion is to drink a cup or two of water thirty minutes before a meal, and then limit beverage consumption during the meal.

Digestion can be delayed if you drink iced beverages at mealtimes. I recommend water without ice.

Do not drink any water at bedtime since it tends to interfere with sleep. I especially do not recommend water at bedtime if a person has an enlarged prostate, a hiatal hernia, or GE reflux disease. (For more information on the beneficial effects of water, I recommend my book, *What You Don't Know May Be Killing You* [Siloam Press, 2000].)

WINE IN JESUS' TIME

During the days of Jesus, wine was a regular part of most everyone's diet, just as bread and water were consumed routinely.

Jesus' first miracle was turning water into wine. Early in the gospel of John, we find the story of Jesus telling the servants at a wedding to fill six large water pots, each of which contained twenty or thirty gallons, with water. Jesus then turned that water into wine. John writes about this miracle: "This beginning of signs Jesus did in Cana of Galilee, and manifested His glory; and His disciples believed in Him" (John 2:11).

Wine was most commonly made from grapes, but it was also made from figs, dates, and even pomegranates.

DID JESUS DRINK WINE?

Many Christians hold to the belief that any wine consumed by Jesus was not fermented. The reason they give is that Jesus was a "Nazirite." The Nazirite vow—which goes all the way back to the Law of Moses—is found in Numbers 6. The specific aspect of this vow related to wine is this:

> Then the LORD spoke to Moses, saying, "Speak to the children of Israel, and say to them: 'When either a man or woman consecrates an offering to take the vow of a Nazirite, to separate himself to the LORD, he shall separate himself from wine and similar drink; he shall drink neither vinegar made from wine nor vinegar made from similar drink; neither shall he drink any grape juice, nor eat fresh grapes or raisins. All the days of his separation he shall eat nothing that is produced by the grapevine, from seed to skin.'" (Num. 6:1–4)

Also as a part of the Nazirite vow, a person was to let the locks of his hair grow. The person under a Nazirite vow was not to go near a dead body, even if it was the body of his father, mother, sister, or brother.

The Nazirite vow was considered to be a vow in which a person was dedicated to special, sacred service. The vow could be made by the individual or by his parents. This dedication, which is called *nazir* in Hebrew, could last for a lifetime or be for only a limited time.

Provision was made for those who had fulfilled their days of separation to make a special offering before the Lord and "after that the Nazirite may drink wine" (Num. 6:20).

The understanding that Jesus lived under a Nazirite vow is drawn from two beliefs, neither of which is clearly stated in Scripture. First, some hold to a belief that Jesus' heavenly Father had set Him aside for a special, sacred service, and therefore, He lived under a Nazirite vow all His life. The second belief is that because Jesus is called a Nazarene in the Scriptures, He was actually a Nazirite. Matthew wrote in his gospel account about Jesus, "He came and dwelt in a city called Nazareth, that it might be fulfilled which was spoken by the prophets, 'He shall be called a Nazarene'" (Matt. 2:23). It should be noted that all those who lived in Nazareth were Nazarenes, but certainly not all who lived there were Nazirites. There is, however, no specific prophecy in the Old Testament that the Messiah would be called either a Nazarene or a Nazirite. The prophets to whom Matthew referred may have been prophets cited in Jewish traditions, or they may have been prophets who were prophesying in the day of Jesus.

One of the people who lived under a Nazirite vow was Samson. In Judges 13 we find this instruction given to Samson's parents even before Samson was born: "Behold, you shall conceive and bear a son. Now drink no wine or similar drink, nor eat anything unclean, for the child shall be a Nazirite to God from the womb to the day of his death" (Judg. 13:7).

There is also mention in the Scriptures of two other people who were dedicated to be Nazirites from before their birth: Samuel (1 Sam. 1:11) and John the Baptist (Luke 1:15). Again, however, there is no mention of Jesus having been dedicated in this way by either His earthly parents or His heavenly Father.

The only thing we can really conclude with certainty about whether Jesus was a Nazirite is this: There is no mention in the New Testament, either on the part of Jesus or the apostles, that Jesus ever took a Nazirite vow, either temporarily or permanently.

No Wine for Priests on Duty

Others point to a Levitical law as evidence that Jesus did not drink fermented wine. In Leviticus we find this command of the Lord to Aaron, the high priest:

> Do not drink wine or intoxicating drink, you, nor your sons with you, when you go into the tabernacle of meeting, lest you die. It shall be a statute forever throughout your generations, that you may distinguish between holy and unholy, and between unclean and clean, and that you may teach the children of Israel all the statutes which the LORD has spoken to them by the hand of Moses. (Lev. 10:9–11)

In the New Testament, Jesus is called our "High Priest" (Heb. 7:26–8:2). Because of this, the assumption is made that Jesus was on duty as a priest during His entire earthly life. In actuality, Jesus did not function as a priest in the tabernacle or the temple. He was from the tribe of Judah, not Levi—in other words, He was not a Levite (Heb. 7:14). He became our High Priest in the aftermath of His crucifixion, resurrection, and ascension.

The commandment given to Aaron and the priests on duty in the tabernacle is a very common-sense approach. A priest who had had too much to drink was a priest whose perception would be clouded. He was a priest who was likely to overlook blemishes, and a priest who was not likely to be thinking straight as he declared the commandments of God. But the commandment not to drink wine did not apply to priests who were off duty.

Kings, by the way, were also advised not to drink wine or intoxicating beverages for this same purpose: their clarity of mind, memory, and judg-ment. We read in Proverbs:

It is not for kings, O Lemuel,

It is not for kings to drink wine,

Nor for princes intoxicating drink;

Lest they drink and forget the law,

And pervert the justice of all the afflicted. (31:4–5)

New Wine?

There are some who believe that the term new wine refers to wine that is the juice of the grape prior to fermentation. There is no basis in either history or Scripture for this claim that new wine was unfermented. New wine technically referred to the current vintage of wine.

Jesus said,

No one puts a piece of unshrunk cloth on an old garment; for the patch pulls away from the garment, and the tear is made worse. Nor do people put new wine into old wineskins, or else the wineskins break, the wine is spilled, and the wineskins are ruined. But they put new wine into new wineskins, and both are preserved. (Matt. 9:16–17)

To understand this passage, we need to understand something about the way wine was made at that time.

Grapes were harvested from the vineyards and then placed in a large vat, where they were trampled with bare feet. This is mentioned in Isaiah 63:3. The juice that was squeezed out of the grapes ran into smaller vats and there it fermented for approximately six weeks. The juice then was placed in goatskin flasks (the "wineskins" of Matthew 9:17) or in jars (as mentioned in John 2:6).

129

The reason new wine was not to be placed in old wineskins was precisely because of its fermenting qualities—new wine was subject to the greatest amount of fermentation, and the gases released as part of the fermenting process were likely to break apart the seams or weak areas of an old wineskin. These words of Jesus had nothing to do with the consumption of a beverage; they referred to the impartation of the Holy Spirit to those who would believe in Jesus as their Savior.

On the day of Pentecost in Acts 2, the disciples were all gathered together. They were then all filled with the Holy Ghost. At the time of Pentecost, Jews came to Jerusalem from various parts of the world and spoke foreign languages. These foreign Jews were confounded because they heard the disciples from Galilee speaking in different foreign languages. However, the Jews from that area of Judea who didn't understand the foreign languages simply mocked, saying, "They are full of new wine" (Acts 2:13). In other words, they thought that the men were drunk and simply speaking gibberish.[1] (New wine was referring to actual wine and not grape juice.)

What we do know with certainty is that Jesus lifted a cup of wine at the Last Supper and said, "This cup is the new covenant in My blood. This do, as often as you drink it, in remembrance of Me" (1 Cor. 11:25). There is no reference whatsoever that this was unfermented wine.

Did Jesus actually drink the cup blessed at the Last Supper? Here is how Matthew records that event:

Then He took the cup, and gave thanks, and gave it to them, saying, "Drink from it, all of you. For this is My blood of the new covenant, which is shed for many for the remission of sins. But I say to you, I will not drink of this fruit of the vine from now on until that day when I drink it new with you in My Father's kingdom." (Matt. 26:27–29)

It appears that Jesus did have wine that night, and that He recognized He would not be drinking wine again with them until after His resurrection. Jesus said He drank wine. He responded to the criticism of the Pharisees and religious lawyers who rejected Him, saying,

> For John the Baptist came neither eating bread nor drinking wine, and you say, "He has a demon." The Son of Man has come eating and drinking, and you say, "Look, a glutton and a winebibber, a friend of tax collectors and sinners!" (Luke 7:33–34, italics added for emphasis)

WHAT KIND OF WINE DID JESUS DRINK?

The wine produced in Israel during the days of Jesus was primarily red wine. Red wine is by far the most common wine produced throughout history.

Red wine has been used in medicine for thousands of years. Hippocrates, the father of medicine, used wine around 400 B.C. to treat numerous ailments including headaches, mood swings, and cardiac irregularities. He also used it as a means to aid digestion, as a sleeping aid, and as a nerve tonic.

Plato stated, "No thing more excellent nor more valuable than wine was ever granted mankind by God." Louis Pasteur echoed this sentiment centuries later in saying, "Wine is the most healthful and most hygienic of beverages."

THE DOCUMENTED HEALTH BENEFITS OF RED WINE

No other food or beverage decreases the overall mortality or the incidence of heart attacks more than wine.[2]

In 1992 a major scientific study was published that awakened the interest of the American medical community to what was called "the French paradox." Scientists Serge Renaud and Michel de Lorgeril published their findings in *Lancet*, the prestigious British medical journal, pointing out these facts: The French consume approximately a third more fat, including saturated fats, than Americans. They smoke more than Americans and exercise very little. Yet they have one of the lowest heart attack rates in the world. They also have one of the lowest incidences of stroke.

These scientists who took a look at the French way of life concluded that this low incidence of heart disease was due to the fact that the vast majority of people in France consume a moderate amount of red wine daily. In fact, the main alcoholic beverage consumed in France is red wine. The scientists concluded that the properties in red wine caused less stickiness of platelets in the blood, which in turn resulted in lower incidences of coronary heart disease.[3]

Subsequent studies found that subjects who drank one to two glasses of red wine a day had a decrease in risk of heart disease of approximately 30 to 50 percent.[4] From the medical research published to date, it is clear that no other single food or beverage decreases the overall mortality from heart disease, or the decreased incidence of heart attacks, more than moderate consumption of red wine.

These results echoed the earlier work of Dr. Arthur Klatsky, a cardiologist, who began studying the link between heart disease and alcohol intake as early as the 1970s. Initially, Dr. Klatsky studied the health records of 80,000 patients. In the end, the ten-year study included 129,000 patients. He found that both men and women who consume moderate amounts of alcohol are significantly less likely to die from heart disease.[5]

Cardiovascular disease accounts for nearly 50 percent of the total annual mortality rate in the United States. Nearly one million Americans a year die from cardiovascular-related diseases. The annual cost of cardiovascular-related procedures—including bypass surgeries, cardiac catheterizations, and angioplasties with stents—is more than $100 billion per year.[6] The average cost of a hospital stay in the aftermath of myocardial infarction (heart attack) is $14,772. The average cost of bypass surgery and hospital stay is $32,346, and the average cost of angioplasty and hospital stay is $21,113.[7]

Help for Ischemic Stroke

The consumption of moderate amounts of red wine has been shown to decrease the risk of developing ischemic stroke. An ischemic stroke is caused by a blood clot, and the flavonoids of red wine—especially quercetin, catechin, epicatechin, and resveratrol—all decrease the clotting tendency of the blood.

Red wines have fifty to one hundred times more resveratrol than white wines. Resveratrol is a substance found in grape skins. It helps prevent fungus from growing on the grape skin. In the human body, resveratrol increases HDL (good) cholesterol and functions as an antioxidant, inhibiting the oxidation of LDL (bad) cholesterol and reducing the amount of plaque that builds up in a person's arteries. Oxidized cholesterol is a main cause of atherosclerosis. Resveratrol also helps prevent blood clots.

Another potent flavonoid in red wine is quercetin, which functions as an antioxidant and an anti-inflammatory. It also helps prevent blood clots by decreasing platelet clumping.

More than a thousand different ingredients and nutrients have been found in red wine. It is especially rich in phenolic compounds, which are the phytochemicals that give wine its bitterness and astringency. In making red wine, the skin of the grape is left mixed in as fermentation occurs; thus, red wine has a much higher phenolic content than white wine. Red wine also has more than one hundred different flavonoids—flavonols, anthocyanins, catechins, and the oligmers and polymers of the catechins.

Flavonoids have antioxidant and anti-inflammatory properties. Apart from quercetin and resveratrol, some of the most common flavonoids in red wine are catechin and epicatechin. Flavonoids as a whole inhibit platelet aggregation, which decreases the risk of blood clots and thereby decreases the likelihood of heart attacks and strokes.

No single phenolic or flavonoid makes red wine protective for the heart. Rather, it is a combination of flavonoids and phenolic compounds that provides protection against cardiovascular disease and stroke. The diverse group of phenolic chemicals and flavonoids functions as a team to raise HDL (good) cholesterol, lower oxidation of LDL (bad) cholesterol, and decrease the stickiness of platelets and fibrinogen (the main component of blood clots).

Help for Cancer

The properties of red wine also seem to have some beneficial properties against cancer. Quercetin, especially, has been found to have powerful anticancer properties.

Help for Digestion

Red wine also helps stimulate digestion. We read in Paul's letter to Timothy: "No longer drink only water, but use a little wine for your stomach's sake and your frequent infirmities" (1 Tim. 5:23). Moderate amounts of red wine stimulate the acid secretion in the stomach without injuring the mucosal lining. (Note: If a person has gastritis or ulcer disease, by all means avoid all forms of alcohol.)

I personally believe one of the reasons the French have less heart disease is not only due to their moderate wine consumption, but also because they make dining an experience. A French meal has multiple courses. A five-course meal is common in France. Such a meal usually includes a small appetizer, a more substantive appetizer, then the main course, and then a fourth course—often cheese—and finally, dessert. Wine is usually consumed at both lunch and dinner. The pace of the meals is relaxed, with ample time between courses to allow for digestion and feelings of satiation. The result is that less food is consumed per course, and the wine aids in efficient digestion.

Not only does wine help to improve digestion, but it helps prevent gastroenteritis and traveler's diarrhea. Dr. Martin Weisse of West Virginia University found that drinking one to two glasses of wine with a meal may also help prevent food poisoning and dysentery. In his research study, red wine outperformed bismuth salicylate, which is the active ingredient in Pepto-Bismol. Both red and white wines were found to be more effective in killing bacteria associated with dysentery than other forms of alcohol.[8]

This may seem like old news to some. In the late nineteenth century, a cholera epidemic broke out in Paris. Those who drank wine generally avoided the dysentery associated with cholera. Frequent travelers abroad have discovered from practice that drinking a glass of red or white wine with each meal is a great antidote for traveler's diarrhea. And actually, in the case of preventing diarrhea, white wine is even more effective than red wine.

Wine is effective in preventing kidney stones. Of twenty-one beverages studied, wine was most strongly associated with the decreased formation of kidney stones in a study conducted by a Harvard research team.[9]

Help for Anxiety

For hundreds of years, wine has been used to treat anxiety, depression, and insomnia. This wisdom goes all the way back to the book of Proverbs:

> Give strong drink to him who is perishing,
> And wine to those who are bitter of heart.
> Let him drink and forget his poverty,
> And remember his misery no more. (Prov. 31:6–7)

Physicians for centuries have prescribed one to two glasses of wine at bedtime for both insomnia and anxiety. Alcohol, however, is a central nervous system depressant, and since alcoholics are prone to depression, I do not recommend any alcohol for anyone with depression. Depression may actually lead to a person becoming an alcoholic.

ARE OTHER ALCOHOLIC DRINKS AS BENEFICIAL?

Many people assume that if red wine is good for a person's physical health, other forms of alcohol are beneficial as well. Not so.

Beer and hard liquor do not have the same health properties. A study called the Copenhagen Heart Study was reported in the *British Medical Journal* in 1996. The study compared those who drank wine, beer, and hard liquor. A 4-ounce glass of wine, a 12-ounce bottle of beer, and a 1.5-ounce shot of 80 proof liquor were compared—the alcohol content of each of these beverages is about half an ounce.

The results were that individuals who drank wine had the lowest incidence of death from heart disease and the lowest mortality rate—in fact, the mortality rate had decreased by 50 percent! But for those drinking equivalent amounts of spirits, the mortality rates actually increased! Beer had no effect on mortality rate.[10]

What Constitutes a "Glass" of Wine?

When we speak of a "glass of wine," we generally are talking about four ounces of wine, or half a cup. That amount is the average amount in a traditional wine glass. In today's society, we find wine glasses that are huge by comparison—sometimes holding twelve or more ounces. Keep in mind that a standard portion of wine—a glass—is only half a cup. In drinking one glass of wine with a meal, a person should be drinking no more than four ounces, or one-half a measuring cup's worth.

The U.S. Department of Agriculture defines moderation in alcohol intake as no more than one drink per day in women and no more than two drinks per day in men. Scientific research bears this out. In fact, a number of studies have been done that demonstrate a relationship between increasing amounts of alcohol and increasing mortality rates.

A research study performed by Harvard Medical School studied more than twenty-two thousand men ranging in age from forty to eighty-four over a ten-year period. Their research concluded that men who consumed two to four alcoholic beverages a week were significantly less likely to die of heart or circulatory disorders. These were surprising results when compared to those of their much more reserved counterparts who drank on average less than one alcoholic beverage a week. Those studied also had fewer cancers over the ten-year period. However, men who consumed two or more alcoholic beverages *a day* experienced a death rate that was 51 percent higher. So there lies the lesson to be learned: Two beverages a week may be beneficial and/or protective, but consuming two beverages a day proved deadly for many involved. Is it worth the risk?[11]

TO DRINK OR NOT TO DRINK: THAT IS THE QUESTION

The National Institute on Alcohol Abuse and Alcoholism (NIAAA) advises: People should not be encouraged to drink for health reasons; and if they do drink, it should not exceed one or two drinks daily.[12]

Many groups of people should avoid all use of alcohol. They include

- pregnant women

- people with liver disease, such as chronic hepatitis or cirrhosis

- people with congestive heart failure, hypertriglyceridemia, or hypertension that is not under control

- people with porphyria

- people with active ulcer disease or gastritis

- people with addictive tendencies

- people with depression

- teens

The Biblical Laws Against Excessive Consumption

From cover to cover, the Bible has strict admonitions against excessive drinking of alcohol. Repeatedly, we find that those who drink in excess experience terrible consequences.

The first person in the Bible who is described as being intoxicated was Noah, who planted a vineyard after the great Flood. In Genesis 9:21, we read that "he drank of the wine and was drunk." His sons discovered him naked in his tent, and the son who "saw the nakedness of his father," Ham, was cursed as a result (9:22, 25).

Lot, the nephew of Abraham, is also cited as a person who had too much to drink. Lot escaped from Sodom with his two daughters—his wife looked back and was turned into a pillar of salt. Lot and his daughters lived isolated and in fear, dwelling in a cave in the mountains above Zoar. As time passed, Lot's daughters conspired, saying, "'Our father is old, and there is no man on the earth to come in to us as is the custom of all the earth. Come, let us make our father drink wine, and we will lie with him, that we may preserve the lineage of our father.' So they made their father drink wine that night" (Gen. 19:31–33).

On two successive nights, these young women caused their father to drink wine, and in his drunken state, he had sex with both of his daughters. Both became pregnant by him. The first daughter delivered a son and named him Moab. The second daughter delivered a son and named him Ben-Ammi. Moab became the father of the Moabites; Ben-Ammi became the father of the Ammonites. The result of this incest was the creation of two groups of people who became the archenemies of the Israelites throughout many centuries (See Gen. 19:36–38).

Proverbs 20:1 says,

> Wine is a mocker,
>
> Strong drink is a brawler,
>
> And whoever is led astray by it is not wise.

In the New Testament, Peter taught against excessive wine consumption. He cited the former lives of those who now knew Christ, and he described that life as a time when the believers "walked in lewdness, lusts, drunkenness, revelries, drinking parties, and abominable idolatries" (1 Peter 4:3). These behaviors were not to be manifested among people in the church.

The apostle Paul wrote to the Ephesians: "Do not be drunk with wine, in which is dissipation; but be filled with the Spirit" (Eph. 5:18).

Many people excuse the act of drinking wine since Jesus drank wine. However, Galatians 5:22–24 says, "But the fruit of the Spirit is love, joy, peace, longsuffering, kindness, goodness, faithfulness, gentleness, self-control. Against such there is no law. And those who are Christ's have crucified the flesh with its passions and desires." To crucify the flesh means to abstain from lustful desires. Temperance is defined as self-control, but it also involves restraints. The restraints are being imposed by you on you. God is not going to restrain you, but is going to leave it up to you to restrain yourself. You will not be able to practice temperance until you are able to restrain the flesh. Paul goes on to say that Christians have crucified their flesh so that the flesh no longer has control over them. Unfortunately, many Christians have not crucified their flesh and are not practicing temperance.

Medical Admonitions Against Excessive Consumption

In Jewish tradition, teens are considered to have come of age at thirteen. They are expected to drink small glasses of wine along with adults as part of their religious services. The rate of alcoholism among Jews, interestingly, is among the lowest rates of alcoholism in the world.[13] Therefore, for most people, I recommend that they lay all alcoholic beverages on the altar and abstain from alcohol until they have crucified the flesh and have the fruit of temperance operating in their lives. Many people, unfortunately, will have to avoid alcohol forever since their flesh is too weak to resist temptation for just one more drink.

Alcohol usually affects the brain of a teen much differently from the way it affects the brain of an adult. The brain doesn't finish developing until an individual reaches their mid-twenties. One of the last areas of the brain to mature is that of the frontal lobes. This area is involved with the capability to make complex judgments and plans. Different areas of mental ability are usually affected by chronic alcohol intake. These include:

· Problem solving: They generally have greater difficulty solving simple problems such as whether to clean the house or run errands. They have even more difficulty with more complex problems such as setting up a new television or computer.
· Forming new memories: They generally have problems forming new memories, but not remembering old information that was learned in the past.
· Problems concentrating: They usually have problems concentrating and focusing their attention.

- Problems with abstract thinking: Abstract thinking is the way we interpret the meaning of events, circumstances, or stories.

- Difficulties with perceiving emotion: A normal person is able to perceive both emotion and attitude in others' speech, whereas a chronic drinker generally has problems in this area.

Consequences of Alcohol Abuse

Heavy consumption of alcohol can have deadly consequences. First, there is an increased risk of numerous diseases. All of the following diseases have been associated with excessive alcohol intake: cirrhosis of the liver; pancreatitis; cancer of the tongue, mouth, pharynx, larynx, esophagus, stomach, pancreas, and liver; breast cancer; weakness of the heart muscle; stroke; high blood pressure; neurological problems; dementia; memory loss; confusion; withdrawal seizures; anemia; bleeding from the gastrointestinal tract; depression; and various forms of psychiatric illness.

Every year in the United States, approximately 100,000 deaths are due to alcohol-related diseases.[14]

Second, excessive alcohol consumption has been linked to increased risk of accidents, homicide, domestic violence, falls, burns, and suicides. According to the National Highway Traffic Safety Administration, approximately half of all fatalities in automobile accidents occur in crashes where either a driver or a pedestrian had been drinking. Sadly, the vast majority of alcohol-related fatalities are innocent people who are pedestrians, passengers, or occupants of other cars.

Third, excessive alcohol consumption can lead to alcoholism. People with a strong family history or a personal history of alcoholism should avoid all forms of alcohol. The most important predictors of alcoholism appear to be alcoholic parents, alcoholic ancestors, and cultural background.[15]

The risk of a man becoming addicted to alcohol increases dramatically if he drinks more than three to four drinks a day. Women need to consume only three alcoholic beverages a day to become addicted.

Alcoholism is characterized by an uncontrolled urge to drink, as well as a tolerance to increasing quantities of alcohol. It is defined by the World Health Organization as "alcohol consumption by an individual that exceeds the limit accepted by the culture or injures health or social relationships." Many alcoholics find they have an uncontrollable urge to continue to drink once they have begun. Alcohol ends up controlling them rather than vice versa. If you find that you have a craving for more than one to two glasses of red wine at a meal—or if you continue to drink more and more wine without even thinking about it—you should seriously face this tendency.

One way to screen whether someone has a problem with alcohol is the commonly used CAGE test. The person must answer these questions:

· Have you ever felt the need to cut down on your drinking?

· Have you ever felt annoyed by someone criticizing your drinking?

· Have you ever felt guilty about your drinking?

· Have you ever felt the need for an "eye opener" (which is a drink at the beginning of the day)?[16]

If an individual answers yes to two or more of the questions, there is a good probability that there is some degree of an alcohol problem.

The very negative consequences of alcoholism are listed as follows:[17]

Increased Mortality

· Mortality rates for alcoholics are double the usual death rate in men, and triple in women.

· Alcoholism is the fourth leading cause of death in men between the ages of twenty-five and forty-five in these four categories: accidents, homicides, suicides, and cirrhosis.

· Alcoholics have a suicide rate that is six times greater than the average population.

· Alcoholics have a ten-year decrease in life expectancy.

Annual Economic Toll

· Lost production for alcoholics: $14.9 billion

· Health care costs: $8.3 billion

· Accident and fire losses: $5 billion

· Cost of violent crime: $1.5 billion

· Total cost to the United States society: $136 billion

BENEFITS OF RED WINE WITHOUT THE ALCOHOL

There are several health alternatives you should consider in place of alcohol. One alternative is to take an extract of the beneficial properties of red wine available in supplement form, which does not contain alcohol.

This supplement, available in a capsule, is marketed under many different brand names. One is called "French Paradox"—others are simply under the name "red wine capsules." The capsules have been standardized as to their content, and they provide the important phytochemicals found in red wine. The capsules are usually less expensive than red wine itself, and they contain no alcohol.

The second alternative to red wine is to purchase nonalcoholic red wine products. These have all the beneficial effects of red wine without the adverse effects associated with alcohol.

Finally, purple grape juice—preferably natural grape juice that has had no sugar added—has many of the same health benefits of red wine. The problem with the consumption of grape juice is that it tends to be overconsumed—more than four ounces—and people often choose grape juice drinks that have been diluted and have a great deal of added sugar.

OTHER BEVERAGES IN JESUS' TIME

In addition to water and wine, a number of teas and juices were likely consumed in Jesus' time. We know, for example, that berries were juiced, as were pomegranates. Mulberries were also crushed to make a refreshing beverage. A number of teas were also made, and were generally used for medicinal purposes more than as a beverage at meals. Mint tea was certainly common then, as it is today. Jesus certainly may have consumed these juices and teas—there is no record of His having done so, however, in the Bible.

WHAT WOULD JESUS DRINK?

Jesus certainly drank water and red wine, and may have drunk various juices and herbal teas as well.

We can follow Jesus' example by making sure that our water is pure, filtered or distilled, and that if we choose to drink red wine, we limit our consumption to only one four-ounce glass a day. I strongly encourage my patients as well as my readers to choose a nonalcoholic red wine substitute, red wine capsules, or a supplement that contains the powerful phytonutrients quercetin and resveratrol.

CHAPTER NINE

WHAT WOULD JESUS EAT FOR DESSERT?

I HEARD RECENTLY ABOUT A MOTHER WHO WAS preparing breakfast for her two-year-old daughter. She asked the toddler, "What would you like for breakfast—a bagel or a bowl of cereal?"

The little girl answered, "Chocolate."

"No," her mother replied. "You can't have chocolate for breakfast. Do you want a bagel or cereal?"

Again the little girl said, "Chocolate."

Slightly exasperated, the mother said, "No, honey. You can't have any chocolate until after lunch. Now what do you want . . . a bagel or cereal?"

The little girl said with a grin, "Lunch!"

From early childhood, it seems, we have a sweet tooth. Sweetness is one of the major tastes registered by the taste buds of the tongue. We tend to feel deprived if we have no sweets at all.

What type of sweets did Jesus eat? What did He have for dessert?

The answer to both questions is simple: fruit.

FRUIT: A STAPLE OF THE ISRAELITE DIET

Fruit was a main staple food of Jesus, just as it had been for the Israelites for thousands of years.

When Moses sent out twelve spies to the land of Canaan, he directed the spies to bring back some of the fruit from the land. In Numbers 13:23 we read,

> They came to the Valley of Eshcol, and there cut down a branch with one cluster of grapes; they carried it between two of them on a pole. They also brought some of the pomegranates and figs.

Talk about a productive vineyard! A cluster of grapes so large that two men were needed to carry it on a pole between them was a very large cluster of grapes!

Grapes, figs, and pomegranates are three fruits mentioned frequently in the Bible. They are fruits that have strong symbolic significance as well as practical uses. Other fruits mentioned in the Bible include apples, apricots, berries, melons, dates, and raisins.

GRAPES ARE A RICH SOURCE OF NUTRIENTS

The Bible has more references to grapes and grapevines than to any other fruit and plant except olives and olive trees.

Grapes are the first cultivated plant mentioned in the Bible. They can be traced all the way back to Noah (Gen. 9:20–21). After Noah left the ark, he planted a vineyard; he went from being a caretaker of animals to a caretaker of vines. Throughout the ages, from July to October each year, fresh, ripe grapes have been eaten along with bread as one of the mainstays of the daily diet of those living in Israel. Grapes become ripe first in the south of the land, beginning in July, and are ripe in the areas north of Galilee as late as October.[1]

Purple and red grapes are rich in anthocyanin, a form of flavonoid that functions as an antioxidant. A family of chemicals known as OPCs include grape seed extract and pine bark extract. These phytonutrients are water soluble, and clinical studies have suggested that they may be fifty times more potent than vitamin E and twenty times more potent than vitamin C in terms of antioxidant activity. OPCs are able to cross the blood-brain barrier, and thus have the ability to protect the brain and spinal nerves from free radical damage. Grape seed extract also helps repair connective tissue and protect the liver from damage from numerous toxins.[2] Grape seed extract may reduce the pain and swelling from varicose veins, as well as revitalize aging skin and decrease bruising of the skin.

Grapes have been shown to fight tooth decay and to stop viruses, and they are high in caffeic acid, a substance shown to be a strong cancer-fighting agent.

Grapes are also a rich source of resveratrol, another powerful phytonutrient. Resveratrol is found in the highest concentrations in red grapes, especially those from cold, damp regions such as France and Canada. It is present in both the grape leaves and the grape skins. Resveratrol is found in highest concentrations in red wine and purple grape juice. White grape juice, white grapes, and white wine have low concentrations of this phytonutrient.

Resveratrol is an antioxidant that helps protect the heart and blood vessels in several ways: it decreases the stickiness of platelets, and it has been shown to help boost good (HDL) cholesterol and block oxidation of bad (LDL) cholesterol. It helps decrease inflammation. Animal studies with resveratrol suggest it also may inhibit the development and progression of cancer.[3]

Finally, resveratrol functions as a Cox-2 inhibitor—when the Cox-2 enzyme is inhibited, cancer activity is reduced, as is inflammation. The benefits are especially important to those who suffer from arthritis.

Yet another phytonutrient in grapes is ellagic acid, which has both antimutagenic and anticarcinogenic properties. It has been shown to inhibit chemically induced cancers of the liver, lungs, skin, and esophagus in rodent studies. Ellagic acid also protects our DNA.[4]

Grapes are high in boron, a mineral known to help ward off osteoporosis. They are also high in potassium and zinc, and the vitamins A, B, and C. And the good news for dieters is that a cup of raw grapes has only fifty-eight calories, only 0.3 grams of fat, and no cholesterol.

The Israelites in ancient times made grape honey, a product similar to our jams and jellies but without artificial preservatives or added sugar. You can make this today by following this simple recipe: Wash four cups of grapes, and remove all stems. Place the grapes in a pan with a half cup of water, and boil the mixture about twenty minutes, or until it thickens. Strain off the grape seeds. Store the mixture in sterilized jars, and refrigerate them. The natural sugars in the grapes become concentrated—the sweeter the grapes were to begin with, the sweeter the grape honey will be.

Grapes were pressed to make not only wine, but also fresh juice and vinegar. Grapes were pressed into cakes of flour, as were raisins. Sour wine and vinegar made from grapes were given to Roman soldiers to prevent diarrhea and help make them strong in battle.[5] As Jesus hung on the cross, He was given sour wine on a sponge of hyssop (John 19:28–30).

RAISINS

In addition to fresh grapes and the juice from grapes, grapes were dried and eaten in the form of raisins.

Researchers at Tufts University have developed a method for analyzing each food to determine its comprehensive antioxidant capacity. Samples of foods are blended into liquid chromatographs, and then they are analyzed as to how quickly and effectively free radicals are quenched when they are added to the mix. The foods highest in antioxidant capacity as a whole were fruits and vegetables. The top two individual foods were prunes and raisins!

In the Old Testament, we read how Abigail gave David a great provision of food, including a hundred clusters of raisins (1 Sam. 25:18). Raisins were also brought to King David as he fled from Absalom (2 Sam. 16:1).

Besides having a high concentration of antioxidants, raisins are a good source of iron, potassium, B vitamins, dietary fiber, and carbohydrates.

A word of warning, however—raisins have a much higher concentration of sugar than does other fresh fruit. They also are subject to more pesticide residue. To avoid problems, I would strongly recommend that you choose organic raisins.

FIGS WERE ABUNDANT IN JESUS' TIME

The fig tree is the first fruit tree actually mentioned by name in the Bible. In Genesis 3, after Adam and Eve had eaten of the forbidden fruit, we read that their eyes were opened, and they knew they were naked. They "sewed fig leaves together and made themselves coverings" (Gen. 3:7).

Figs are one of the seven plants mentioned in Deuteronomy 8:7–10, the passage of Scripture in which God describes the abundance of the promised land:

> For the LORD your God is bringing you into a good land, a land of brooks of water, of fountains and springs, that flow out of valleys and hills; a land of wheat and barley, of vines and fig trees and pomegranates, a land of olive oil and honey; a land in which you will eat bread without scarcity, in which you will lack nothing; a land whose stones are iron and out of whose hills you can dig copper. When you have eaten and are full, then you shall bless the LORD your God for the good land which He has given you.

For centuries, various nations and cultures around the world have regarded figs as a powerful remedy for ailments ranging from cancer to constipation, scurvy to hemorrhoids, gangrene to boils, liver troubles to menopausal symptoms.

When King Hezekiah was sick to the point of death, he was visited by the prophet Isaiah, who gave him this word from the Lord: "Set your house in order, for you shall die and not live" (Isa. 38:1).

Hezekiah turned his face to the wall and prayed to the Lord and wept, reminding the Lord that he had walked before Him in truth and with a loyal heart, and had done what was good in the Lord's sight. The Lord sent Isaiah back to Hezekiah with this word, "I have heard your prayer, I have seen your tears; and I will add to your days fifteen years. I will deliver you and this city from the hand of the king of Assyria" (Isa. 38:5–6). Isaiah also gave this advice: "Let them take a lump of figs, and apply it as a poultice on the boil, and he shall recover" (Isa. 38:21).

Figs have been used throughout the ages to help fight skin cancers. Figs, as well as the extract from figs, contain benzaldehyde. Japanese researchers, especially, have experimented with benzaldehyde derived from figs as a treatment for cancer patients, and their results are impressive.

Also in the Bible, David's men once found an Egyptian warrior who had been without food and beverage for three days and nights. We read that "they gave him a piece of a cake of figs and two clusters of raisins. So when he had eaten, his strength came back to him" (1 Sam. 30:12).

Figs have high amounts of fiber, magnesium, potassium, calcium, manganese, copper, iron, and vitamins C and B6. Figs have been recommended for centuries to tone and nourish the intestines.

In Bible times, figs were usually eaten as dried figs, and were often pressed into cakes. But here is a warning—dried figs are quite high in sugar, and they have a laxative effect. I do not recommend that a person eat an excessive quantity of figs at one time!

Fresh figs range in color from deep purple-black to golden yellow. When you purchase them fresh, they should be fragrant, firm, and without any soft or brown spots. Dried or fresh, figs keep best in the refrigerator. If you are buying dried figs, be sure to check what may have been added to them. Some people are allergic to sulfites, which are often used to preserve dried figs and other dried fruits.

In Bible times as well as today, an arrangement of dried fruits is a popular dessert. Dried figs, apricots, and raisins can be soaked overnight and then gently boiled with a piece of cinnamon. They can later be served cold with a little orange or lemon juice.

Jesus and a Fig Tree

It was customary in Bible times for people who traveled about the land on foot to eat fruit from trees that were along the roadside. They were trees that grew wild and were uncultivated.

At one point in Jesus' ministry, He and His disciples were hungry, and they spotted a fig tree in the distance. But as they got closer to the tree, they found no fruit on the tree—only leaves. Jesus cursed the fig tree, and He and His disciples continued on to Jerusalem. The next morning, as they passed by the same tree, the disciples noticed that the tree had dried up from the roots. (See Mark 11). It is customary for fruit and leaves to appear simultaneously on fig trees in Israel—the lack of fruit meant that the tree was not fulfilling its purpose as a tree. Jesus likened the lack of productivity of the tree to the lack of true spiritual growth and life in those who rejected Him.

Jesus certainly wasn't opposed to either fig trees or figs. He was opposed to any aspect of creation not fulfilling its intended purpose.

POMEGRANATES ARE POPULAR IN ISRAEL

Pomegranates have been growing in Israel for thousands of years. They are among the fruits brought back by the twelve spies sent out by Moses.

Pomegranates are rich in color, but they are also considered to be one of the most difficult fruits to eat due to the large quantity of seeds inside each piece of fruit. According to Jewish tradition, there are 613 seeds in a fully mature pomegranate—the same number as the number of laws God gave to Israel.[6]

However, the pomegranate has sweet, juicy fruit, and one of the best ways to eat the fruit is fresh, slowly sucking the fruit from each seed.

Pomegranate juice is also available; it is usually called "grenadine." A refreshing drink is made in the Middle East using pomegranate juice and carbonated mineral water.

Pomegranates are high in potassium as well as vitamins B and C, copper, and magnesium. Pomegranates are a good source of fiber.

APPLES AND APRICOTS?

Did Adam and Eve actually eat an apple from an apple tree? That question has been asked for hundreds of years.

In Genesis 2:17, we read God's admonition that Adam and Eve not eat from the Tree of the Knowledge of Good and Evil in the Garden of Eden. In Genesis 3, however, the serpent tempted Eve to eat from this tree, and we all know the rest of the story. Eve ate the forbidden fruit and then gave it to Adam, who also ate. Both of them were consequently banned from the Garden of Eden.

For centuries, people have assumed that the fruit that Adam and Eve ate was an apple, since that was the translation given in old English texts. It is very unlikely, however, that the fruit was the apple as we know it in the United States because there are no apple trees native to that area of the world.[7]

It is neither likely that apples as we know them are the fruit called "apples" in the Song of Solomon (Song 2:5; 8:5). It is much more likely that the fruit in question was either pomegranates or bitter oranges.

This does not at all mean, however, that we should avoid eating the apples with which we are familiar. The very opposite is true! Unpeeled apples are high in pectin, a special form of fiber that has been shown to lower cholesterol levels, bind and eliminate toxins from the GI tract, and help relieve constipation. Fresh apples contain phytonutrients including ellagic acid, which, as noted previously, possesses significant anticancer properties. Those who eat apples regularly have been shown to have far fewer colds and upper respiratory infections than those who do not. The old saying, "An apple a day keeps the doctor away," has a great deal of medicinal truth to it!

The only way, however, to get the maximum nutrition from an apple is to eat the apple unpeeled. Most of the phytonutrients are destroyed by cooking the apples for applesauce or apple juice. I recommend that you purchase organically grown apples to avoid the pesticides, chemicals, and waxes that are often found on apples.

Researchers at Michigan State University have called the apple "the all-around health food."

Apples have been shown to

- lower LDL (bad) cholesterol and high blood pressure

- fight viruses

- stabilize blood sugar

- suppress the appetite without robbing the body of necessary nutrients, which is of help especially to those who are attempting to lose weight

- regulate bowel function, preventing constipation or helping treat diarrhea, depending upon a person's need

- prevent tooth decay

- help stop the growth of cancer cells

A person who eats two or three apples a day can greatly boost the body's protection against heart disease. One study conducted in France concluded that a diet heavy in apples actually lowered heart-damaging cholesterol levels from 28 to 52 points, without any other significant changes in eating or exercising habits!

Apricots

Proverbs 25:11 says, "A word fitly spoken is like apples of gold in settings of silver." Apricots are known as golden apples.

For centuries, the people in the mountainous countries of the Himalayas have traditionally eaten large amounts of a wild apricot known as the *kubani*. They attribute their good health and long life to this fruit.

Dried apricots may be even better for us than raw fruit. And there's good news for dieters—one apricot has only seventeen calories and a mere 0.4 grams of fat while providing more than half the recommended supply of vitamin A.

Apricots are abundant in the Holy Land. They are high in carotenes including beta carotene, potassium, magnesium, and iron. The apricot pits contain amygdalin, otherwise known as B_{17} or laetrile. Amygdalin is found in many other foods including the seeds of apples, cherries, peaches, and plums. It is also found in millet and buckwheat. Amygdalin is a compound composed of two sugar molecules, hydrogen cyanide and benzaldehyde. According to some scientists, apricot pits can either cure or kill. A study at the Mayo Clinic showed that patients can actually develop symptoms of cyanide poisoning since laetrile is able to form cyanide in the body.

Cancer treatment with laetrile is illegal in the United States; those who seek this treatment generally go to clinics in Mexico. Some of the clinics there have reported great success in treating a wide variety of cancers. A large clinical study performed at the Mayo Clinic and sponsored by the National Cancer Institute using laetrile, however, did not find any beneficial effects of laetrile for those with advanced cancer.

Still other researchers claim that there are benefits from eating the raw, natural ground-up pits of apricots, as well as the pits and seeds from other seed-bearing fruits. Their recommendation is that fruit be eaten whole—skin, fruit, and seeds or pits—and that there are great health benefits in eating the whole of a fruit, as opposed to ingesting only one part of it.

More studies need to be done in this area, specifically in the use of laetrile; we need to determine definitively the safety and effectiveness of laetrile.

BERRIES HAVE IMPORTANT BENEFITS

Berries are also mentioned in Scripture, especially the fruit of the mulberry tree (See 2 Sam. 5:23–24; 1 Chron. 14:14–15). The fruit of the mulberry tree resembled large blackberries. Black mulberries were commonly eaten fresh or were juiced. They have been used for centuries in the making of jam or jelly, and to make wine.

Berries such as blueberries and blackberries also have a high antioxidant capacity. In fact, blueberries and blackberries are third and fourth on the list of potent antioxidant foods (after prunes and raisins).

Berries—especially blackberries, blueberries, raspberries, and strawberries—are rich in flavonoid phytonutrients. The phytonutrient called anthocyanin is actually responsible for the rich colors of the different types of berries. Berries also contain the important phytonutrient ellagic acid.

MELONS AND CUCUMBERS

Melons are another of the foods that the Israelites craved from their days of living in Egypt. Some Bible historians believe that these melons were watermelons, which continue to grow profusely along the banks of the Nile and in various other regions of Egypt. Others believe the melons were muskmelons, or what we know as cantaloupes in the United States.

The muskmelon has sometimes been called the "Queen of Cucumbers." Many people believe the cucumbers mentioned in the Bible are actually melons, including the "garden of cucumbers" in Isaiah 1:8. If you remove the seeds from cucumbers, you will likely find that the fruit of a peeled cucumber is virtually indistinguishable from a melon as an ingredient in a fruit salad. It is the rind and the seeds of cucumbers that give them their distinctive taste—and their gaseous effects.

The good news is that melons of all types have good nutritional benefits! Cantaloupes are an important source of carotenoids—the beta carotene in cantaloupe is converted to vitamin A, which helps to stimulate the immune system. Beta carotene also works as an antioxidant, and it helps to stimulate T-helper cells, which are very important to immune function. Studies have repeatedly shown that diets high in carotenoids help decrease the likelihood of developing several types of cancer.

Cantaloupe also has ingredients that act as anticoagulants (blood thinners), which may explain the correlation between cantaloupe and the prevention of cardiovascular disease.

Watermelon contains the powerful carotenoid lycopene, which is responsible for its red pigment. Foods high in lycopene have been shown to help prevent prostate cancer. Watermelon has one of the highest water contents of all fruits—if you dislike drinking water, you may try eating more watermelon to keep your body adequately hydrated. Watermelon is also an excellent diuretic.

In eating watermelon and other water-rich fruits and vegetables, you need to make certain that they have not been grown in an area that uses sewage as fertilizer. This is especially true when it comes to eating melons grown in developing countries. Many tourists have become ill from eating melons grown in areas where raw sewage was used to fertilize crops.

DATES ARE STILL POPULAR IN ISRAEL

Date palm trees have been growing in Israel since the earliest biblical times. The palm has always flourished in the desert, and it tends to be an indicator in the desert that water is near. Date palms still flourish along the seacoast of Israel, in the Galilee region, and in the deserts.

Psalm 92:12 tells us, "The righteous shall flourish like a palm tree." This is a reference to the longevity, fruitfulness, and usefulness of the palm. The date palm is a tree that has multiple beneficial uses—virtually every aspect of the tree has a direct use for humans.

Dates grow in clusters. A cluster may have as many as two hundred dates and weigh up to twenty-five pounds. Dates are very sweet and succulent. They are a rich source of minerals and fiber. Perhaps their only detriment is that they are high in sugar. In fact, their sugar content is about 60 to 70 percent.

It was the fronds of the date palm that the people waved as they welcomed Jesus to Jerusalem, crying, "Hosanna! Blessed is He who comes in the name of the LORD! The King of Israel!" (John 12:13).

OTHER FRUITS GOOD FOR HUMAN HEALTH

The Bible has hundreds of references to plants, and we certainly cannot cover them all in a couple of chapters. Many fruits were not common to Israel but are very good for human health, such as pineapple and citrus fruits. Certainly you need not limit your consumption of fruit to only those named in the Bible.

I recommend that you eat a variety of fruits in your diet, making sure to eat at least two to four servings of raw fruit each day. Eating such a diversity of fruits will help you get all the different phytonutrients your body needs, and give you maximum benefit from these phytonutrients in preventing cancer, heart disease, and a variety of other degenerative diseases.

People who consume the most fruits and vegetables usually have the lowest rates of cancer, hypertension, heart disease, diabetes, and arthritis.

The U.S. Department of Agriculture recommends a person eat three to five servings of vegetables a day, and two to four servings of fruit a day.

AS SWEET AS HONEY

Perhaps because it is so sweet, honey is a major symbol for the abundance of God's blessings in the Bible. Instead of processed sugar, people in Bible times used natural honey as a sweetener or ate the honeyed pulps of fresh fruit.

One of the more famous references to honey in the Bible refers to a time of battle between the Israelites and the Philistines. The Bible says:

> Now all the people of the land came to a forest; and there was honey on the ground. And when the people had come into the woods, there was the honey, dripping; but no one put his hand to his mouth, for the people feared the oath. But Jonathan had not heard his father charge the people with the oath; therefore he stretched out the end of the rod that was in his hand and dipped it in a honeycomb, and put his hand to his mouth; and his countenance brightened. Then one of the people said, "Your father strictly charged the people with an oath, saying, 'Cursed is the man who eats food this day.'" And the people were faint. But Jonathan said, "My father has troubled the land. Look now, how my countenance has brightened because I tasted a little of this honey. How much better if the people had eaten freely today of the spoil of their enemies which they found! For now would there not have been a much greater slaughter among the Philistines?" (1 Sam. 14:25–30)

Jonathan, Saul's son and the friend of David, certainly knew from experience that honey, rich in sugar, was a high-energy fuel for the body.

As the story in 1 Samuel progressed, the people were so faint that in the end, they rushed on the spoil they took from the Philistines and slaughtered sheep, oxen, and calves and ate them with the blood. In doing so, they sinned not only against Saul's oath, but also against the Law of Moses regarding clean and unclean foods (14:31–33).

An ancient Egyptian scroll lists approximately nine hundred treatments for a wide variety of illnesses and injuries. More than five hundred of the treatments have honey as a primary ingredient.

The Greeks and Romans knew that honey rubbed into wounds served as a rapid and effective healer. Honey actually can kill dangerous bacteria on the inside as well as outside of the body.

International travelers often take honey with them; it seems to work many times when nothing else does to put a stop to diarrhea. Researchers have found that honey also may be effective in combating pathogenic bacteria which can cause food poisoning such as salmonella, shigella, E. coli, and even cholera!

Proverbs 24:13 says,

> My son, eat honey because it is good,
> And the honeycomb which is sweet to your taste.

In his book *Folk Medicine*, published in 1958, D. C. Jarvis suggested that honey should be used as a treatment for coughs, cramps, burns, and congestion. He also wrote, "A tablespoon of honey at the evening meal" was an effective way of fighting insomnia.[8]

Note: The Centers for Disease Control caution parents of young children *not* to give honey to a child under the age of one year. The reason is that botulism bacterial spores can stick to honey. The immune system of adults is mature and strong enough to fight off such attacks, but very young children are not able to do so.

A single serving of honey, about one tablespoon, has sixty-four calories and seventeen carbohydrate grams. Because honey is high in calories and carbohydrates, we do well to heed the advice of Proverbs 25:16:

> Have you found honey?
> Eat only as much as you need,
> Lest you be filled with it and vomit.

For thousands of years, serving honey has been a way of honoring guests. It generally was served after the main meal at the end of the day.

A common dessert even today in the Middle East is "honey cream." A quarter to a half cup of honey is added to a pint of plain yogurt, sour cream, or heavy cream. Generally speaking, both honey and yogurt (or sour cream or heavy cream) are put in bowls on the table, and each guest mixes his own dessert to taste. On cold nights, the yogurt or cream may be heated slightly; in the summer months, the yogurt or cream is chilled.

NUTS FOR DESSERT

In the Middle East, nuts are far more commonly served as a dessert than they are as an appetizer!

Nuts, such as almonds, pistachios, and walnuts, were plentiful in Jesus' day, and they were often used as ingredients in desserts. Nuts, we now know, are beneficial in regulating blood sugar and lowering cholesterol when consumed in moderation.

Solomon had a "garden of nuts." Many believe this was a grove of walnut trees, since walnuts were highly prized in ancient Israel for the oil they produced. Walnut oil was considered only slightly inferior to olive oil. The walnuts themselves were considered to be a delicious treat. Kings frequently had groves of almond, walnut, and pistachio trees along with their olive and fig tree groves. Walnuts were so highly prized that they were called the "royal" nut.

When Judah sent his sons, including Benjamin, back down to Egypt, he said this: "Take some of the best fruits of the land in your vessels and carry down a present for the man—a little balm and a little honey, spices and myrrh, pistachio nuts and almonds" (Gen. 43:11). He didn't know at the time, of course, that he was sending these items to his own son Joseph.

Nuts have been associated with cancer prevention, a lower risk of heart disease, and help for diabetes.

Here's a quick comparison of three of the most popular nuts available today:

	Almonds (blanched)	Peanuts (dry-roasted)	Walnuts
Per one-ounce serving:			
Calories	174	164	172
Fat grams	16	14	17.6
Carbohydrate grams	9.5	6	3.4
Potassium	95 mg	180 mg	
Magnesium			57.4 mg
Protein grams	1.0	6.6	6.9

Nuts are rich in important minerals such as zinc, iron, copper, calcium, magnesium, and phosphorus. They are also high in protease inhibitors, substances some consider to be the most significant natural cancer blockers yet discovered. All kinds of nuts seem to have protease inhibitors—pistachios, peanuts, walnuts, almonds, Brazil nuts, cashews, acorns, chestnuts, and hazelnuts. Peanuts are not true nuts but are actually a legume.

Nuts are also loaded with polyphenols, which researchers are associating with cancer prevention. Polyphenols appear to tackle cancer cells before they begin to spread uncontrollably throughout the body.

Nuts help to stabilize blood sugar levels—which is good news for diabetics. Peanuts especially seem to permit a slow, steady rise in both blood sugar and insulin.

For centuries in Israel, nuts have been a gift that signifies peace and goodwill. *Kibbet,* which means "treat" in Hebrew, is a mixture of dates, figs, raisins, and nuts. It is often offered to visitors or is served at the end of a meal with honey, yogurt, and tea.

A very common dish served at the Passover meal is *Haroset.* It is a dish that symbolizes the mortar that the Hebrew slaves used in building Pharaoh's pyramids. Haroset is made by combining three-fourths cup of chopped almonds, walnuts, or other nuts with three cups of chopped apples, a half cup of raisins, a half cup of chopped dates, a half teaspoon of cinnamon, and three-fourths cup of grape juice or red wine.

SAYING "NO, THANK YOU" TO DESSERT

Some people find it helpful to remember a couple of key Bible passages as they say "no" to dessert:

Do you not know that you are the temple of God and that the Spirit of God dwells in you? If anyone defiles the temple of God, God will destroy him. For the temple of God is holy, which temple you are. (1 Cor. 3:16–17)

When you sit down to eat with a ruler,
Consider carefully what is before you;

And put a knife to your throat
If you are a man given to appetite.
Do not desire his delicacies,
For they are deceptive food. (Prov. 23:1–3)

Never apologize for not eating dessert—you will be sending a subliminal message to your own self that it is wrong for you to say no. Rather, offer a simple, yet gracious, "no." You will be helping retrain your own mind that you can give up certain foods in order to have a healthier body.

Certainly I'm not opposed to an occasional treat on a special holiday or as part of a celebration. But the key word there is *occasional.* Begin to say no to a daily indulgence of sweets or desserts.

I am not advocating that you say no to desserts and sweets with an air of self-righteousness or pride. A simple, polite "no" will suffice—no sermon or condemnation for others. Your refusal, however, may be just the help an overweight person near you needs in order to refuse dessert also.

Once I had a patient who had a habit of eating a half gallon of ice cream every night before he went to bed, and then he wondered why he weighed more than three hundred pounds and suffered from high blood pressure, high cholesterol, and coronary heart disease. I told him to look on the positive side that he wasn't yet a diabetic! This man made one major behavioral change in his life—he gave up ice cream—and he lost weight.

Now, if you do slip up and eat a bowl of ice cream, or have a candy bar or bag of chips, don't punish yourself by vowing to fast, diet severely, or skip meals. Simply start over with resolve that you are going to make the right choices and eat the foods that Jesus ate. Everyone stumbles occasionally or eats too much of the wrong food. Mistakes are inevitable. Just refuse to make them a pattern or to compound the mistake by continuing to make wrong choices.

For dessert, say "yes" to fruit and occasionally to nuts and a little honey. For snacks, say "yes" to fruit.

Eat your fruit whole, including the skin when it is edible.

Eat your fruit fresh.

Enjoy these alternatives to high-sugar, empty-calorie desserts!

In my experience, the more fresh fruit you eat, the more you will find most other desserts to be too sweet and even sickeningly sweet. It takes a little time, but your taste buds can be retrained.

WHAT WOULD JESUS EAT?

Jesus ate a great deal of fruit, some nuts, and some honey.

We do well to eat more fresh, whole fruit daily, and occasionally to treat ourselves to nuts and a little honey mixed into yogurt or drizzled on fruit.

CHAPTER TEN

DID JESUS EXERCISE?

MANY CHRISTIANS SEEM TO BELIEVE THAT EXERCISE is of very little value. They base their opinion, in part, on what the apostle Paul wrote to Timothy: "Bodily exercise profits a little, but godliness is profitable for all things" (1 Tim. 4:8).

However, biblical times were vastly different from today with regard to people's need for additional "bodily exercise." When Jesus walked the earth, most people walked from three to ten miles a day in the course of their daily lives and work! The people did not need to engage in additional exercise. Extra exercise was usually only done in the Roman Empire to increase muscle size and strength for participation in spectator sports. Certainly Paul valued physical health; he simply believed that getting bodily exercise for the purpose of engaging in sports was not as profitable as using one's time and energy to develop spiritual strength.

When Jesus was approximately four or five years old, He walked with His family from Egypt to Nazareth, a distance of more than four hundred miles. His ministry was marked by frequent travels to various parts of Israel, many of the trips being ones from the Galilee region to Jerusalem, a distance of about 120 miles.

The Jews had seven official feasts—three of which were to be celebrated in Jerusalem: Passover (Feast of Unleavened Bread), Pentecost (Feast of Weeks), and Succoth (Feast of Tabernacles). Exodus 34:23 said of these feasts: "Three times in the year all your men shall appear before the LORD," which meant a visit to the tabernacle or temple.

Being a devout Jew, Jesus' earthly father, Joseph, would have attended these three annual feasts in Jerusalem. It was customary to take one's entire family on these pilgrimages. These trips meant walking through mountainous and desert regions, often in temperatures that might range from freezing (in the fall and early spring) to more than 110 degrees Fahrenheit (in the summer). Jesus very likely made this trip to Jerusalem three times a year from the age of five until the age of thirty. If so, He walked at least 18,000 miles just on these three annual pilgrimages from Galilee to Jerusalem!

We certainly know that Jesus made the trip from Nazareth to Jerusalem when He was twelve years old. In the gospel of Luke we read:

His parents went to Jerusalem every year at the Feast of the Passover. And when He was twelve years old, they went up to Jerusalem according to the custom of the feast. (Luke 2:41–42)

Evangelist Arthur Blessitt once obtained maps that showed the roads Jesus traveled. He calculated that the total miles Jesus walked during the three years of His public ministry were 3,125 miles. He added this mileage to the mileage from Egypt to Nazareth, as well as the miles Jesus walked from Galilee to Jerusalem, and he came up with a total of 21,595 miles that Jesus likely walked during His life.

On many days, it appears that Jesus walked between ten and twenty miles. We have no idea how many miles Jesus may have walked while in the wilderness for forty days at the outset of His ministry. The actual miles Jesus walked in His life may have been double the amount calculated by Blessitt.

As a comparison, the distance around the world at the equator is 24,901.55 miles. It is not difficult to assume that Jesus walked almost the distance around the world in His lifetime![1]

THE MOST BENEFICIAL
EXERCISE: AEROBIC

The most beneficial cardiovascular activity is aerobic exercise. *Aerobic* simply means "in the presence of air." Aerobic exercise both challenges and increases the oxygen-carrying capacity of the body. The cardiovascular system and the muscles become more efficient and stronger. The heart is able to pump out more oxygenated blood per beat, so the heart becomes more efficient and the resting heart rate becomes slower. A slow, strong heart rate is a good sign of cardiovascular fitness. I commonly see marathon runners whose heart rates are fifty beats per minute.

Aerobic exercises are those exercises that use the large muscle groups of the body in repetitive motions for a sustained period of time. These exercises may include brisk walking, jogging, aerobic dancing (including jazzercise), cycling, swimming, rowing, stair-stepping, skating, and cross-country skiing. An aerobic effect can also be gained by playing a vigorous game of racquetball, singles tennis, basketball, or another active sport.

Even moderately paced walking is an excellent form of aerobic exercise. In fact, some research shows that moderately paced walking five times a week for thirty minutes is just as advantageous as brisk walking or jogging, although the benefits from a brisk walk or jog can be achieved in less time.

As an active walker, Jesus certainly was engaged in aerobic exercise.

THE HEALTH BENEFITS OF AEROBIC EXERCISE

The greatest benefit of aerobic exercise is that it significantly decreases the risk of cardiovascular disease. In fact, the risk can be decreased by approximately 50 percent. For those with heart disease, aerobic exercise lowers the risk of the disease progressing. Aerobic exercise results in the body forming collateral circulation in the coronary arteries. These additional arteries act as something of a natural bypass, and they improve the circulation to the heart muscle.

Aerobic exercise also decreases what are called *coronary risk factors*. These are factors that seem to impact heart disease. Aerobic exercise helps decrease body weight, lower blood pressure, lower blood triglyceride levels, and lower LDL (bad) cholesterol. Regular aerobic exercise also helps raise HDL (good) cholesterol. In one study, researchers monitored more than 84,000 female nurses for eight years. Those women who exercised regularly had a 54 percent decreased risk of both heart attack and stroke when compared to sedentary women. Similar studies with men have produced similar results.

Exercise also helps prevent diabetes and improve glucose tolerance, which is the body's ability to regulate the level of sugar in the blood. Impaired glucose tolerance often leads to diabetes. About one in four adults in our nation at present is at risk of developing impaired glucose tolerance and eventually diabetes. Exercise also improves the body's ability to use insulin.

Recent studies reveal that regular physical activity significantly decreases the chance of developing adult onset diabetes even if one doesn't lose weight. However, weight loss will further reduce one's risk of diabetes. People who exercise regularly decrease their risk of Type II diabetes by nearly 300 percent![2] Approximately 90 percent of all diabetics have Type II diabetes. This form of diabetes is not a true insulin deficiency, but a resistance of tissues, especially liver and muscle tissue, to the effects of insulin.

Regular aerobic exercise also helps decrease the risk of developing cancer. Individuals who are physically active have a dramatically decreased risk for developing colon, breast, and prostate cancer.[3] So many people are concerned today about these three types of cancer, and perhaps the best thing they can do to prevent them is to lace up their walking shoes and go for a brisk walk four or five times a week! What is good for the body is also good for the soul—getting a little fresh air and sunshine is good for you!

THE HEALTH VALUE OF WEIGHT-BEARING EXERCISE

Weight-bearing exercises, which include jogging, aerobic dance, and walking, also help a person maintain bone density and thereby prevent osteoporosis.[4]

Osteoporosis is very common in women over the age of fifty. Bone mass decreases at an annual rate of 0.3 to 0.5 percent usually after the age of thirty. This loss increases to approximately 2 to 3 percent when a woman goes through menopause, and this rate of loss occurs for about ten years thereafter. Over their lives, women tend to lose about 35 percent of their cortical bone mass (the long bones of their arms and legs), and about 50 percent of their trabecular bones (vertebrae). Men, in comparison, lose only about a quarter of their cortical bone mass and only about a third of their trabecular bone mass over the course of their lives.[5]

Dr. Kenneth Cooper, considered to be the founder of the aerobics exercise movement, is a strong advocate for impact-type exercises, which increase bone density in both men and women in skeletal areas that are subjected to the increased pressure from impact exercises. Exercises that fall into this category are aerobic dance, skipping rope, canoeing, volley-ball, jogging, and tennis.

EXERCISE AND WEIGHT CONTROL

One out of two Americans is either overweight or obese. Obesity is a risk factor for heart disease, hypertension, diabetes, arthritis, some forms of cancer, and other degenerative diseases.

Walking is one of the best aids to weight loss known. Brisk walking helps a person both reach and maintain the ideal body weight in two ways: by increasing muscle mass and basal metabolic rate, and by decreasing appetite.

How does exercise impact a person's metabolism, and what does this have to do with weight control? The basal metabolic rate of a person decreases by about 5 percent for every decade of life after the age of twenty. Sedentary individuals have a significant decrease in their muscle mass as they age. In sedentary individuals, there is approximately a seven-pound loss of muscle mass every ten years past the age of twenty. Regular aerobic exercise, as well as weight training, helps a person increase muscle mass and thus raise the body's basal metabolic rate. As the metabolic rate goes up, a person is better able to lose weight. Because both metabolic rate and muscle mass decrease as we age, it is very difficult for a person to prevent weight gain after middle age unless that person exercises on a regular basis.

Additionally, aerobic exercise has been shown to decrease a person's appetite and also decrease cravings for foods.

OTHER BENEFITS OF REGULAR EXERCISE

Certainly exercise promotes psychological well-being. Exercise reduces stress and anxiety by enabling a person to burn off the stress chemicals that fuel anxiety. It increases the release of endorphins in the brain; endorphins are hormonelike substances that elevate mood and give a person a sense of well-being.

One of the benefits of maintaining your ideal weight is psychological. A person who has improved muscle tone and is at an ideal weight is a person whose appearance is usually good, which creates a favorable self-image. Improved cardiovascular capacity gained through regular exercise increases a person's energy level and promotes more restful sleep. Better rest and higher energy are a great combination for generating a positive outlook on life!

Aerobic exercise is best done from midafternoon to early evening. I recommend that people walk, jog, or engage in aerobic exercise at least an hour before their evening meal to help release the tensions of the day, suppress their appetites, and give energy for the evening's activities. People who engage in aerobic exercise too late at night may find that they have too high an energy level to fall asleep readily. For weight reduction, it is usually best to perform weight training exercise prior to the aerobic exercise.

Another extremely important result of aerobic exercise is related to the lymphatic system, a system about which many people know very little. When the heart pumps blood, the blood follows two routes. One route is through the circulatory system of arteries and veins, and the other is through the lymphatic system. The lymphatic system has very small vessels that are present in all tissues and usually run alongside small veins and arteries. The small lymphatic vessels contain about fifteen liters of lymph fluid; in other words, there is about three times more lymph fluid in the body than actual blood.

The lymphatic system is extremely important in eliminating toxins from the body, and also in maintaining the body's immune defenses. The lymphatic system includes the lymph nodes—every person has about six hundred lymph nodes that act as filters. The white blood cells in the lymph nodes scan the lymphatic fluid for bacteria, viruses, organic debris, and other microbes. The white blood cells include macrophages, T-cells, B-cells, and lymphocytes, which attack the viruses, fungi, and bacteria. A very large part of the lymphatic system—at least 60 percent—is in the intestines, especially in the intestinal walls. When the lymphatic system is sluggish or blocked, white blood cells are slowed down or prevented from killing viruses, bacteria, and other microbes. As a result, disease can more readily take root in the body.

Whereas blood serves primarily to feed the cells oxygen and nutrients, the lymphatic fluid functions to remove cellular waste. Lymphatic fluid circulates much more slowly than blood—in fact, it makes a full circuit through the body usually only once a day.

Lymphatic fluid is composed of approximately 50 percent plasma protein, and the lymphatic system is the major system for carrying blood plasma protein throughout the body. When the lymphatic system is impaired, protein—which is the essential building block for all cells—is unable to get to all of the body's cells efficiently. The plasma protein in the lymphatic system is about half of all the plasma protein circulated in the body. After circulating through the body in the lymphatic system, the plasma protein is passed back into the bloodstream. The lymphatics clear out lipoproteins, such as dangerous LDL (bad) cholesterol, and other toxic substances from circulation.

Lymphatic fluid enters the bloodstream or lymphatic system at the thoracic duct, which is in the left upper chest region. When the lymphatic fluid backs up, or becomes stagnant due to infection or lack of exercise, the whole system can become toxic because of the failure of the lymphatics to dispose of cellular waste.

How does the flow of lymphatic fluid relate to exercise? The lymphatic system works differently from the blood circulatory system. The circulatory system depends upon the heart pumping blood. The lymphatic system, which actually flows upward against gravity in all areas of the body except the head and neck, depends upon muscle contractions for adequate flow. Muscle contractions actually push the fluid through the lymphatic channels. If activity level decreases, the flow of the lymphatic fluid is much more sluggish. Aerobic exercise can increase lymphatic flow threefold! That means three times the amount of cellular waste, foreign microbes, arterial plaque, and LDL (bad) cholesterol is removed.

A more rapid flow of lymphatic fluid also means that proteins are more readily recirculated into the bloodstream. When these proteins back up in the lymphatic system, they tend to attract water. The result is often swelling or edema in different tissues of the body.

Some of the best aerobic activities to stimulate lymphatic flow seem to be jumping rope and jumping on a minitrampoline.

Yet another advantage of exercise is that it increases perspiration, which is another method for the body to rid itself of waste products. Perspiration helps keep the skin clean and supple, and it also regulates the temperature of the body. Perspiration may not be fashionable, but it's healthy! We live in air-conditioned homes, work in air-conditioned offices, drive in air-conditioned cars, and shop in air-conditioned malls. We wear antiperspirants to keep us from perspiring. Most Americans live a sedentary lifestyle that discourages perspiration. The result is a buildup of toxins in the bodies of most Americans—toxins that are clearly associated with a wide variety of degenerative diseases.

I believe one of the reasons God created the summer was so that man could perspire out of his system many of the poisons that had accumulated during the fall, winter, and spring seasons.

The skin has been called "the third kidney" by some in the medical field because it is able to release toxins such as pesticides, solvents, heavy metals, urea, and lactic acid from the body. Approximately 99 percent of perspiration is water, and the remaining 1 percent is generally toxic waste. Brushing the skin with a loofah brush or any rough brush can help remove dried skin that accumulates on the epidermis. I recommend dry skin brushing prior to taking a shower. This brushing can help improve excretion of toxins by unclogging sweat pores and increasing circulation.

Exercise not only increases perspiration, but it also improves circulation to the skin, which brings nutrients to nourish the skin and remove cellular waste products. The nutrients to the skin help repair and rejuvenate the skin, usually causing a more youthful appearance.

Exercise has many other health benefits, including improving digestion and elimination. Regular exercise coupled with adequate water intake can increase the frequency of bowel movements by promoting peristalsis. Exercise also lowers the risk of developing blood clots. In summary, few things can do more to promote good health than adequate physical activity, and especially exercise that is aerobic.

STARTING AN EXERCISE PROGRAM

In starting an exercise program, the most important exercise that almost everyone can perform on a regular basis is walking. The only equipment required is a good pair of walking shoes. But if you don't enjoy walking, find an exercise that you do enjoy. By doing what you enjoy, you are likely to engage in the exercise more often and for a sustained amount of time. If you prefer to ride a bicycle, dance, skate, hike, swim, or engage in another aerobic activity, do so.

Dr. Kenneth Cooper recommends twenty to thirty minutes of aerobic activity three to four days a week.[6] I recommend that my patients schedule a half-hour appointment three to four days a week for exercise. Write it down in your day planner or on an appointment calendar. Then keep the appointment!

One of the interesting findings coming out of exercise research is that the thirty minutes of exercise a day do not need to be done at the same time—a fifteen-minute walk at the start of the lunch hour and a fifteen-minute walk an hour before dinner result in similar benefits to a thirty-minute concentrated period of exercise.

You will probably find it much easier to maintain an exercise program if you are accountable to another person. Recruit a family member or friend to exercise with you regularly, or join an exercise group or class. The important thing is to start, and then to continue exercising on a regular basis. Make exercise a priority.

Determine Your Exercise Heart Rate Range

In starting an exercise program, you need to determine your exercise heart rate range. Your target heart rate should be between 50 and 80 percent of your maximum heart rate. To determine this range, subtract your age from 220. Multiply that number by .5 (50%) and then multiply that number by .8 (80%). Here's an example: a forty-year-old person would subtract 40 from 220 (220 − 40 = 180); 180 x .5 = 90; 180 x .8 = 144. The exercise heart rate range is 90 to 144 beats per minute.

As you begin your exercise program, keep your heart rate range between 50 and 60 percent of the maximum. In the example, that would be between 90 and 108 beats per minute. After a couple of months, increase the intensity to 60 to 70 percent of the maximum. In the example, that would be between 108 and 126 beats per minute. After several more months, and as you become more physically fit, increase the intensity of your exercise to 70 to 80 percent. Again, in our example of a forty-year-old, that number would be 126 to 144 beats per minute.

Increasing your heart rate beyond 80 percent of the predicted maximum is actually more harmful than beneficial. The main reason is that exercise causes more free radicals to be produced in the body. The good news is that under normal conditions and in the healthy ranges described, more antioxidants are also produced in the body to take care of the increase in free radicals. However, those individuals who exercise too intensely or for too long a period can produce excessive amounts of free radicals. This excessive amount of free radicals can damage tissues and organs.

Dr. Kenneth Cooper has addressed this problem in his book *Antioxidant Revolution*. He discusses the dangers of overtraining and especially the overtraining done by many marathon runners. Those who consistently overtrain at a high intensity actually increase their risk of developing cancer, heart disease, and other degenerative diseases.[7] I strongly recommend that you not become a "weekend warrior"—a person who exercises only on weekends. Weekend warriors usually operate under the assumption that thirty minutes of exercise four to five times a week are equal to two to three hours of solid exercise on a weekend. That assumption is false!

Weekend warriors have more pulled muscles, aches and pains, shin splints, foot problems, and other musculoskeletal problems than regular exercisers. Weekend warriors are not the only people, of course, who overtrain or overexert. The risk of a heart attack for a sedentary fifty-year-old male after strenuous physical activity like shoveling snow is greater than 10,000 percent, compared to an individual of the same age who exercises regularly and is well conditioned.[8]

Most exercise physiologists and physicians, including Dr. Kenneth Cooper, recommend that a person undergo a thorough medical exam prior to starting an exercise program. That medical exam, in Dr. Cooper's opinion, should include an exercise treadmill test conducted by a qualified physician. This is especially recommended for persons over thirty years old and for those who have any cardiovascular risk factors.

It is important to add stretching exercises as well as resistance exercises to your aerobic exercise. Stretching promotes flexibility and can also serve as a good warm-up prior to exercise, which helps prevent musculoskeletal injuries. Stretching can also help reduce symptoms of arthritis.

Resistance exercise—also called weight training—is especially important to preserve muscle mass and prevent osteoporosis.

If you are starting a walking program, I strongly recommend you stretch prior to walking, and start your walk slowly to warm up your muscles. Increase your pace gradually. Slow your pace a few minutes before the end of your walk as a cooldown. This pattern can significantly decrease your risk of injury.

DOING WHAT YOU KNOW TO DO

Life expectancy in the United States is fast approaching eighty years, and the number of elderly individuals is growing at twice the rate of the remainder of the population. Every year in the United States more than a million people have heart attacks, and more than 500,000 people will die from heart disease. Researchers at the Centers for Disease Control estimate that 250,000 deaths every year can be attributed to lack of exercise.

Being totally sedentary predisposes a person to a 55 percent increased risk of dying early, in comparison to those who engage in light to moderate regular activity. More than 90 percent of our population agree that regular physical exercise is good for our health, but only about 20 percent of adults are active on a regular basis. We simply don't do what we know to do.[9] Many people have memberships in health clubs that they do not use, or they have stationary bicycles or Nordic Tracks stored in their garages. The 1990s was a boom decade for the exercise industry, with many health clubs springing up, more home exercise equipment being manufactured than ever before, and an increased interest in exercising with personal trainers. But often what we begin as an exercise program appears *not* to be what we sustain.

The greatest admonition for exercise is this: Start.

The second greatest admonition is this: Exercise regularly.

And the third greatest admonition is this: Keep exercising.

When it comes to exercise: Do what you know to do. And keep doing it and doing it and doing it.

WHAT WOULD JESUS DO?

In the case of exercise, we need to do what Jesus did: Get ample exercise daily. For most people, the most beneficial exercise is walking, which is the way Jesus got His exercise on this earth.

CHAPTER ELEVEN

USING THE FOODS JESUS ATE TO LOSE WEIGHT

YEARS AGO I ATTENDED A CONVENTION AT A VERY large hotel in Las Vegas. When my wife and I arrived in the dining room for breakfast, we found an enormous room with lavishly decorated tables that seemed to contain every imaginable food. On one side of the room were foods in their "natural states." There were fresh fruits in abundance—mounds of grapes, freshly cut pineapples, grapefruit, cantaloupe, honeydew, peaches, nectarines, oranges, apples, and colorful displays of strawberries, raspberries, and blueberries. This side of the room also had a table of whole-grain cereals and breads, as well as nuts, seeds, and yogurts.

But on the opposite side of the food buffet were man-made and cooked foods: pancakes, waffles, doughnuts, pastries, eggs, hash browns, sausage, bacon, biscuits, gravy, and other high-fat, high-sugar, processed foods.

We sat in full view of both large displays. I told my wife to notice what type of person tended to walk to each buffet table. She became engrossed in this activity and started keeping score. In the end, we could conclude with strong anecdotal evidence—if not clinical scientific data—that the typical person who ate from the high-sugar, high-fat table tended to be overweight, with more puffiness around the face and eyes, and generally stooped shoulders and a more sallow complexion. These people tended to appear more tired, with a lower general energy level.

On the other hand, the people who chose food from the table with fruits, whole grains, seeds, nuts, and yogurt seemed to be thinner and more energetic, had better complexions and posture, and seemed all around healthier in appearance.

That was an eye-opening experience for my wife. From that day on, she began to eat more fruits, vegetables, whole grains, seeds, and nuts. We drastically reduced our intake of fast food, junk food, and highly processed foods. We not only improved our physical appearance, but our energy levels also soared. By choosing to eat the foods that Jesus ate, we turned our diet of empty, useless, and often disease-aiding calories into calories full of health-promoting vitamins, phytonutrients, antioxidants, minerals, fatty acids, and enzymes.

LOSING WEIGHT ON THE FOODS JESUS ATE

Eating the foods that Jesus ate is very simple. There's no counting of calories, fat grams, or carbohydrates. Eating the Mediterranean diet regularly over time and increasing one's level of activity, including daily walking or exercise, will gradually result in weight loss.

If a person has a weight problem, however, there are specific steps that can be followed to enhance weight loss:

1. Limit starches to only one serving per meal. Choose whole grains and beans over processed starches.

2. Limit consumption of olive oil to one to two tablespoons with each meal. If you are making a dressing for a green leafy lettuce and fresh vegetable salad, use only one to two tablespoons of olive oil with balsamic vinegar and other spices. Request salad dressing on the side and lightly dip the salad in the dressing. Eliminate all other cooking oils, lards, and butter. If you must have oil in a spreadable form for bread, mix equal parts of olive oil and well-softened butter, then allow the mixture to recool in the refrigerator. Have only one small pat of olive oil butter per meal.

3. Limit consumption of fish or poultry to two portions a day—each portion only two to four ounces. Have only one serving of free-range beef or other red meat a week—no more than three to four ounces.

4. Begin your lunch and dinner meals with a large, fresh, dark-green lettuce salad (to which you may want to add other fresh vegetables). Take your time eating the salad. You'll find it much easier to say no to starches or meat dishes that may follow on the menu.

5. Limit red wine to only two or four ounces while you are trying to lose weight.

6. Choose to eat your fruit as whole fruits, not as juice. Have a piece of fruit in the morning, and then use fruit as a snack or dessert. Apples are very filling and can really take the edge off the need for sweets. As you are losing weight, avoid the higher-glycemic fruits such as bananas, dates, figs, mangoes, papaya, raisins, prunes, or kumquats. Instead, choose apples, blackberries, blueberries, raspberries, strawberries, cantaloupes, grapefruit, grapes, honeydew, kiwifruit, nectarines, oranges, peaches, pears, pineapples, plums, tangerines, and watermelon.

The good news is that a Mediterranean diet adapted for weight loss can include as many nonstarchy vegetables as a person desires: salad greens, broccoli, cabbage, asparagus, green beans, spinach, zucchini, kale, turnip greens, squash, and cauliflower, among others.

A NATIONAL EPIDEMIC OF OBESITY

We have an epidemic of obesity in the United States. In fact, the United States has the highest rate of obesity of any nation in the industrialized world. More than half of all American adults are either overweight or obese, and approximately 25 percent of our children are either overweight or obese.

The body mass index, or BMI, is a reasonably accurate estimate of body fat. Underwater weighing is a much more accurate measure of body fat. However, determining the BMI is much more practical and easy. The equation for determining BMI is:

$$\text{Body mass index} = \text{weight in kilograms/height m2}$$

Since we in America don't deal in kilograms and meters, let me put that into plain "American" for you by providing you with a handy chart.

A BMI of 18.5 to 25 is considered normal weight. Anything under 18.5 is underweight. A BMI of 30 to 35 is obese, and anything over 35 is considered severely obese.

THE BASIC PRINCIPLE FOR ALL WEIGHT LOSS

All weight loss is based upon a very simple principle: eat fewer calories than you burn. You can accomplish this by either eating fewer calories

BMI	19	20	21	22	23	24	25	26	27	28	29	30	31	32	33	34	35
Height (inches)	Body Weight (pounds)																
58	91	96	100	105	110	115	119	124	129	134	138	143	148	153	158	162	167
59	94	99	104	109	114	119	124	128	133	138	143	148	153	158	163	168	173
60	97	102	107	112	118	123	128	133	138	143	148	153	158	163	168	174	179
61	100	106	111	116	122	127	132	137	143	148	153	158	164	169	174	180	185
62	104	109	115	120	126	131	136	142	147	153	158	164	169	175	180	186	191
63	107	113	118	124	130	135	141	146	152	158	163	169	175	180	186	191	197
64	110	116	122	128	134	140	145	151	157	163	169	174	180	186	192	197	204
65	114	120	126	132	138	144	150	156	162	168	174	180	186	192	198	204	210
66	118	124	130	136	142	148	155	161	167	173	179	186	192	198	204	210	216
67	121	127	134	140	146	153	159	166	172	178	185	191	198	204	211	217	223
68	125	131	138	144	151	158	164	171	177	184	190	197	203	210	216	223	230
69	128	135	142	149	155	162	169	176	182	189	196	203	209	216	223	230	236
70	132	139	146	153	160	167	174	181	188	195	202	209	216	222	229	236	243
71	136	143	150	157	165	172	179	186	193	200	208	215	222	229	236	243	250
72	140	147	154	162	169	177	184	191	199	206	213	221	228	235	242	250	258
73	144	151	159	166	174	182	189	197	204	212	219	227	235	242	250	257	265
74	148	155	163	171	179	186	194	202	210	218	225	233	241	249	256	264	272
75	152	160	168	176	184	192	200	208	216	224	232	240	248	256	264	272	279
76	156	164	172	180	189	197	205	213	221	230	238	246	254	263	271	279	287

Source: National Heart, Lung, and Blood Institute

than your body is burning or by increasing your activity level to burn more calories than you are presently consuming.

Two of the most popular diets in America are the low-carbohydrate diets such as the Atkins Diet and the Sugar Busters Diet and the very low-fat diets such as the Pritikin and Ornish Diets. The trouble with these diets is that they set up a person for a binge response, and they have a failure rate of nearly 100 percent after five years, according to the National Institutes of Health Technology Assessment Conference Panel.[1]

Both low-carbohydrate and low-fat diets can work. People lose weight temporarily. However, they nearly always regain the weight they have lost, and many times, they regain even more weight.

One of the main reasons the Atkins Diet and other low-carbohydrate diets work is that they effectively lower insulin levels. Americans eat way too much sugar and processed foods that are high in high-glycemic-index carbohydrates. Both sugar and high-glycemic carbohydrates increase insulin, which in turn lowers sugar levels in the blood and promotes the storage of fat. By eating the foods that Jesus ate, a person eats only very small amounts of sugary foods on rare occasions. In place of high-glycemic processed carbohydrates, a person eats whole-grain starches. Consuming whole grains, beans, legumes, and other high-fiber foods, coupled with the use of olive oil, prevents elevated insulin levels, which in essence "turns off" the signal for the body to store fat.

Low-carbohydrate diets are almost always high in the wrong kinds of fats (such as saturated fats, excessive polyunsaturated fats, and hydrogenated fats). These fats, when used in cooking, create free radicals that cause degenerative damage at the cellular level. Those who follow these diets usually consume excessive amounts of meat and animal fat, which are associated with increased risk of both heart disease and cancer. They usually do not consume enough fruits, vegetables, and fiber, and therefore, these diets are usually deficient in phytonutrients, antioxidants, and fiber, all of which help prevent cancer and heart disease.

The low-fat diets, such as the Pritikin and Ornish Diets, also work. People lose weight. However, the low-fat diet doesn't taste as good, and after eating a meal, a person often leaves the table without feeling satisfied. This can lead to binge eating. For all of these diets, an equal and opposite "binge response" seems to be waiting around the corner.

In sharp contrast, eating the way Jesus ate becomes a lifestyle in which dining is an experience. Foods cooked in olive oil and different herbs and spices are bursting with flavor and are satisfying. Whole, fresh foods, fruits and vegetables, and whole grains leave a person feeling full.

I always encourage a person who desires to lose weight simply to focus on eating the foods that Jesus ate—rather than eating man-made processed foods. Rather than make it a compulsive habit to count carbohydrate grams, fat grams, or calories, concentrate instead on making the right food and cooking choices.

INCREASING YOUR METABOLIC RATE

Another important factor in weight loss is metabolic rate. "Basal metabolic rate" is defined in Stedman's Medical Dictionary as the "heat production of an individual at the lowest level of cell chemistry in the waking state or the minimal amount of cell activity associated with the continuous organic functions of respiration, circulation, and secretion." Basal metabolic rate, in other words, is the rate at which your body functions when you are awake and doing nothing.

Basal metabolic rate must be determined first thing in the morning, before breakfast, when the body and mind are still at rest, in a room with a not-too-cold and not-too-warm temperature.

One of the key regulators for metabolic rate is the thyroid gland. Hypothyroidism is simply low thyroid function. Many people tend to develop hypothyroidism as they age. This condition is diagnosed in two ways—either a low level of thyroid hormone in the blood or an elevated level of the pituitary hormone TSH in the blood.

Before the use of blood tests, it was common to diagnose hypothyroidism based on basal body temperatures. This functional test was developed by Dr. Broda Barnes.[2] You can conduct this test yourself: Record your temperature upon awakening every morning for three to seven days, or even longer. Use a mercury thermometer that you keep by your bed before going to sleep. Upon awakening, place the thermometer under your armpit for ten minutes and then record your temperature. Postmenopausal women may perform this test on any day, but menstruating women should perform the test on the second, third, and fourth days of menstruation. Basal body temperatures of less than 97.6 may indicate hypothyroidism.

Other symptoms of hypothyroidism include depression, menstrual problems, constipation, dry skin, problems losing weight, fatigue, cold sensitivity, and headaches.

What does metabolic rate have to do with maintaining and increasing lean body mass? A great deal! Lean body mass, which is one's muscle weight, is more metabolically active than adipose or fatty tissue. In other words, at rest a pound of muscle burns many more calories than a pound of fat. Most people who need to lose weight actually need to replace pounds of fat with pounds of muscle. This is most effectively and efficiently done through exercise.

Those who exercise regularly, and especially those who walk regularly and also do calisthenics, weight-training, or resistance-training exercises, are those who increase their percentages of muscle in the body. Long after a brisk walk, the metabolic rate remains elevated. And the result is that even at rest, a person tends to have a higher metabolic rate. The higher the metabolic rate, the more fat is burned, and the easier it is to maintain weight loss.

A person can increase metabolic rate by lifting weights (even hand weights at home) or performing calisthenics or other resistance exercises a few times a week and then walking briskly for twenty or thirty minutes.

We tend to think of exercise as something that young people do, but the truth is this: It is even more important for a person to exercise after the age of twenty and to never stop exercising. The basal metabolic rate decreases by about 5 percent for every decade past age twenty. The average woman loses approximately seven pounds of muscle for every ten years past the age of twenty, largely owing to a sedentary lifestyle. It is very easy for a woman to gain weight, even if she doesn't change her eating pattern, and especially so around the menopausal years. As hormone levels begin to decrease, muscle mass also decreases as fat accumulates. Women in the premenopausal period—which may last from five to ten years and may begin as early as the mid thirties—tend to gain an average of two to three pounds a year and sometimes more. During the premenopause period, estrogen tends to be elevated, and that elevation promotes fat storage, especially in the buttocks, hips, and thighs.

During the perimenopausal period (the period of time right before menopause or the year or two before, during and after menstrual cycles end), estrogen and progesterone seem to wax and wane, testosterone levels tend to increase, and all of these factors lead to an even greater storage of fat in the abdomen. Add to that sluggish thyroid function, a decrease of muscle mass, and what seems to be an increase of stress for many women at this time of life, and weight gain seems almost inevitable. Stress, by the way, results in increased levels of serum cortisol and lower serotonin levels. Prolonged high cortisol levels can lead to an increased accumulation of fat around the waist, as well as elevated blood fats and blood sugar.

Lower serotonin levels affect mood and appetite. Low serotonin levels can lead to depression, anxiety, insomnia, and cravings for certain foods, especially sugars and starches. It's easy to see how many people, women especially, get trapped in a vicious cycle that results not only in weight gain, but mood swings and increased cravings for sugars and starches.

To avoid this vicious cycle, begin to exercise regularly and to do a variety of aerobic exercises, calisthenics, and weight-training exercises. Also have your physician check your thyroid function with blood tests, and check your basal body temperature. And then, eat as Jesus ate.

FOOD SENSITIVITIES AND ALLERGIES IMPACT WEIGHT LOSS

Another factor that should be considered when discussing weight loss and the maintenance of weight loss is food sensitivity. More and more Americans are becoming sensitive or allergic to various foods, to a great extent because we overconsume junk foods, fast foods, and highly processed foods with countless additives.

One of the symptoms of food sensitivity, as well as food allergies, is a tendency to gain weight easily, retain fluid readily, and experience more bloating, flatulence, and gas, often with accompanying abdominal cramps, nausea, constipation, diarrhea, fatigue, puffiness and dark circles under the eyes, excessive mucus, mood swings, irritability, and headaches.

Some of the most common food allergies or sensitivities are to dairy products, eggs, wheat, corn, yeast, soy, and sugar. Many people become addicted to these foods both physiologically and psychologically, and they crave the very foods to which they are allergic or sensitive! By craving and overeating these foods, a person can develop a food addiction.

The best way to discern if you have a food allergy or sensitivity is to eliminate the most common food allergens from your diet completely. Simply stop eating all dairy products, eggs, wheat, corn, yeast, soy, and sugar. Then add these food items back to the diet one by one, for a period of time, and observe if any of the common symptoms mentioned occur.

Once a food sensitivity or allergy has been identified, a person must avoid these foods for at least three months. The best way to avoid them, of course, is to avoid processed man-made foods and to eat a natural diet consisting of unprocessed foods, fresh produce, and whole grains. If you suspect or discover that you are sensitive to wheat, substitute millet, brown rice bread, or other nonwheat grains for wheat bread. If a person is sensitive to wheat, he is usually also sensitive to oats, barley, and rye. By eliminating the food to which you are sensitive for three months, you can usually overcome the food sensitivity and are able to add this food back to your diet in small quantities every three to four days.

If you are sensitive to dairy products, you can replace dairy in your diet by eating soy cheese, rice cheese, or other natural nondairy cheese. After ninety days of completely avoiding dairy products, you can usually reintroduce dairy to your diet, consuming it only every three or four days.[3]

BEHAVIORAL MODIFICATION FOR SUSTAINING WEIGHT LOSS

Weight loss and sustained maintenance of weight loss require behavioral modification. Here are ten behaviors that are well worth modifying:

1. Modify the way you shop for and cook food. Many people have difficulty modifying the way they eat. Instead, I recommend they modify the way they shop for food and cook it!

One of the simplest and most effective behavioral strategies is this: Keep all junk food, processed food, and tempting foods out of your grocery cart and out of your house. Don't buy these foods. If you don't have them readily available, you aren't going to be as tempted to eat them.

Many parents tell me that they believe their children will feel neglected if they don't have cookies, chips, or ice cream available for them. I simply tell them to buy their children fresh fruit. They'll quickly adapt and learn to enjoy fruit more than they enjoy ice cream, cookies, chips, and other junk foods.

2. Modify your eating time. Try to eat your evening meal so that you are completely finished with the meal before 7:00 P.M., and do not eat any late-night snacks.

3. Modify your after-dinner activity. Choose to go for a walk after you clean up the dishes from dinner. Enjoy the evening air. Go with your family or a friend, and continue your dinner-table conversation as you walk. You'll find it an enjoyable alternative to plopping down in front of the television.

4. Only have one helping of each food item, and practice "portion control" on that helping. Serve your plate from the serving bowl on the counter or the pot on the stove, and take your plate to the table to eat. You'll be less tempted to go back for a second helping.

5. Start leaving a few bites of food on your plate rather than cleaning your plate. If you add up all the uneaten bites over the course of a month, you are likely to have several meals' worth of food! Many of us were taught as children to clean our plates so we wouldn't waste food, especially with all the millions of starving children around the world. I discovered as a young adult that cleaning my plate never did help those starving children, and that the extra food I was eating was actually going to "waist"—as in *my* waist.

6. Space your meals approximately four hours apart, and don't skip meals. Skipping meals tends to decrease metabolic rate. It also leads to low blood sugar, which usually triggers cravings for sugars, starches, and junk food.

7. Keep healthy snacks around—fruit, nuts, seeds. Have a light, healthy snack prior to doing your grocery shopping.

8. When you go to the grocery store, shop the perimeter of the store. I find that in most grocery stores, most of the healthy foods are located on the outside walls of the store. Avoid the bakery. And refuse to go down the aisle that has chips, cookies, or other tempting foods that are unhealthy.

9. Say "no" to dessert. Don't order any when you go out. If you are offered dessert by a hostess, simply say "no" politely.

10. Finally, refuse to eat food for any reason other than to fuel your body and enjoy a meal with family or friends. Too many of us were given comfort foods as children—they tended to be puddings, soft drinks, and sugary foods. We can associate high-sugar, high-fat foods with happy times (for example, cake and ice cream at birthday parties). The result is that many adults turn to these so-called "comfort" foods when the stresses of life become overwhelming. In loneliness or in times of anxiety, they turn to food to cure what they feel emotionally. Refuse to fall into that pattern.

When you are feeling stressed out or anxious, go for a brisk walk. When you are feeling lonely, call a friend, and better yet, have that friend go on a brisk walk with you!

CHAPTER TWELVE

THE MEDITERRANEAN HEALTHSTYLE

WE HAVE HEARD THE WORD *LIFESTYLE* A GREAT DEAL in the last thirty years. But when it comes to eating the way Jesus ate, I prefer the word *healthstyle*. There's much more to eating the way Jesus ate than simply eating. A good healthstyle requires choices in the foods we buy, choices in how we prepare those foods, and choices regarding exercise and creating a pleasant dining experience for ourselves.

As I hope you will have concluded by the time you are reading this chapter, the best Source for all healthstyle issues is Jesus Christ. His operational manual, the Holy Bible, needs to dictate the way we approach every area of life.

The foods that Jesus ate are very similar to the foods advocated in the very popular Mediterranean Diet of recent years, with the exception of the forbidden foods listed in the books of Leviticus and Deuteronomy. The Mediterranean Diet allows pork and shellfish, as well as fish without scales and other foods forbidden in the Bible. Apart from these variations, the eating plan features foods that were common in Bible times and in the land where Jesus lived.

I am a strong advocate for the Mediterranean Diet as a whole. It is not only a good diet for weight loss, but it is an excellent way to eat for the rest of a person's life. Numerous research studies have indicated that it is the healthiest diet in the world.

The Mediterranean Diet has been followed for centuries by people living around the Mediterranean Sea—variations of the diet are followed in southern France, parts of Italy and Spain, parts of North Africa such as Morocco and Tunisia, and parts of the Middle East including Lebanon, Syria, Israel, and parts of Turkey. Plant sources make up the core of the diet, and the variations in the diet tend to be related to the unique plants found in the various nations.

THE RESEARCH BASIS FOR THE MEDITERRANEAN DIET

The benefits of the Mediterranean Diet have been known for almost forty years, so the long-term impact of this diet is well documented. The diet initially came from the research of Ancel Keys, M.D., and his associates. As early as 1958, Dr. Keys published his belief that a link existed between diet and coronary artery disease. Specifically, he believed in a direct relationship between an increased intake of saturated fats and an increased risk of coronary artery disease. His opinion stemmed from his scientific observation that during wartime food rationing, the consumption of meats and dairy products in some countries in Europe decreased dramatically, and so did deaths from heart disease and overall mortality rate. Among the wealthy people in these nations—those who continued to consume fatty meats and dairy products—the risk of heart disease increased.

Dr. Keys and his researchers studied more than twelve thousand men between the ages of forty and fifty during the years from 1958 to 1964. These men were divided into sixteen study groups in seven nations: the United States, Finland, Japan, Italy, Greece, the Netherlands, and Yugoslavia. Dr. Keys's study became called the "Seven Countries Study."[1]

Each participant in the study was interviewed, examined physically, and had information recorded about his blood pressure, cholesterol level, smoking history, activity level, dietary habits, and several other health habits.

At the end of the study period, Dr. Keys and his researchers analyzed their data on these men and discovered that those in the Mediterranean groups had the lowest mortality rates from all causes. Most surprising to the researchers was the dramatic reduction in the mortality rate from coronary heart disease. The Greek men had the lowest mortality rate overall, and also the lowest rate of heart disease—a rate even lower than that of the Japanese. Finnish men had the highest rate of heart disease, and they also consumed almost 40 percent of their calories from fat, and more than 50 percent of these fat calories were from saturated fat. In comparison, the Greek men consumed almost the same amount of calories from fat, but only a small percentage of their fat calories was from saturated fat. The majority of the fat intake in Greek men was monounsaturated fat, which they tended to consume in the form of olive oil.

The Japanese only consumed 9 percent of their total calories from fat, and only 3 percent from saturated fat, yet the Greeks had a lower incidence of heart disease than the Japanese. Also, the heart disease rate in the Greeks was almost 90 percent lower than those measured in the United States group.

The big question for Dr. Keys and his associates was this: How can a people eat a higher percentage of calories from fat, smoke more cigarettes, drink more wine, exercise very little, and yet have a longer life expectancy, a significant reduction in coronary heart disease, decreased incidence of cancers (other than lung cancer or cigarette-related cancers), and a decreased incidence of hypertension, obesity, and most other degenerative diseases than Americans have? The answer: the components of the traditional Mediterranean Diet.

As we have discussed earlier, the American diet is too high in saturated fats, sugar, processed foods, salt, red meat, and fast foods—and conversely, too low in fresh fruits, vegetables, and whole grains. The Mediterranean Diet has a much better balance.

TWO VERY DIFFERENT
FOOD GUIDE PYRAMIDS

You may find it interesting that in 1991, numerous health organizations demanded that the USDA abandon the four food groups and recommend a significant reduction in sugar, fat, and food oil consumption. They also recommended that the USDA classify dairy products and red meats as optional foods, not one of the four basic food groups. Certainly this recommendation was backed up by numerous scientific research studies that provided conclusive evidence that the high intake of dairy and meat products was a major contributing factor to the development of heart disease, cancer, diabetes, obesity, and a number of degenerative diseases. The next year, the USDA came out with the food guide pyramid to replace the four food groups.

The food guide pyramid shows that the largest portion of our diet— that part making up the base—should consist of bread, cereal, rice, and pasta, which should comprise between 30 and 45 percent of a person's diet. In my opinion, what the USDA did not say—and should have emphasized—is that these foods need to be whole-grain products.

The next level up on the food guide pyramid is the vegetable and fruit

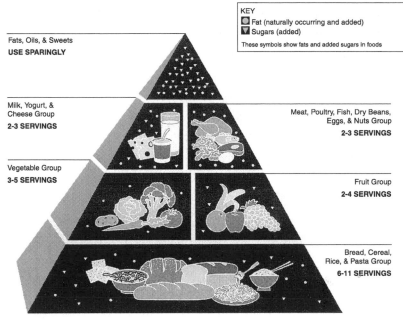

KEY
○ Fat (naturally occurring and added)
▼ Sugars (added)
These symbols show fats and added sugars in foods

Fats, Oils, & Sweets
USE SPARINGLY

Milk, Yogurt, &
Cheese Group
2-3 SERVINGS

Meat, Poultry, Fish, Dry Beans,
Eggs, & Nuts Group
2-3 SERVINGS

Vegetable Group
3-5 SERVINGS

Fruit Group
2-4 SERVINGS

Bread, Cereal,
Rice, & Pasta Group
6-11 SERVINGS

Source: USDA and DHHS

group. Here the USDA recommended three to five servings of vegetables a day, and two to four servings of fruit a day. Vegetables should comprise 15 to 20 percent of a person's daily diet, and fruit should comprise 10 to 15 percent of a person's diet. Unfortunately, the average American seems to think that the three main vegetables to consume are French fries, onion rings, and ketchup, and that fruit should be eaten in the form of jelly, sugar-loaded fruit juice, or out of a can. For the USDA food guide pyramid to be most beneficial, a person should consume whole, fresh fruits and vegetables whenever possible.

The third level up on the USDA food guide pyramid is two to three portions of milk, yogurt, or cheese a day, and two to three servings a day of meat, poultry, fish, dried beans, eggs, and nuts. According to the Food Guide Pyramid, dairy foods should total no more than 10 percent of a person's daily food intake, and meat, beans, eggs, and nuts should also total less than 10 percent of a person's food intake. The USDA sets the portion size for this part of the pyramid at two to three ounces, which gives the impression that a person can consume up to nine ounces of red meat a day. That, in my opinion, is a very unhealthy amount. I do not recommend over 4 ounces of meat a day (preferably poultry and fish).

Fats, oils, and sweets are at the top of the pyramid, and this section is allocated 5 percent of a person's diet. This small section of the pyramid should include all fats and oils, including the oil in salad dressings, cooking oil, fast foods, and processed foods. Most Americans are way over that amount.

The USDA food guide pyramid is a good start, but it doesn't provide adequate clarification for each level of the pyramid. In contrast, here is the food guide pyramid for the Mediterranean Diet.

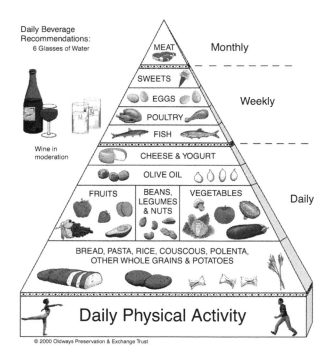

© 2000 Oldways Preservation & Exchange Trust

The Mediterranean Diet emphasizes unprocessed foods. Complex carbohydrates are at the base. These foods include brown rice or whole-grain rice, whole-grain pasta, and whole-grain bread—ideally, all should be prepared fresh daily without preservatives. Other grains appropriate for the base of this pyramid are bulgur wheat (cracked whole wheat), couscous, polenta (coarse cornmeal), and potatoes. Whole-grain breads consumed in Mediterranean nations have a high amount of fiber without excessive sugars, hydrogenated fats, or food additives. In Mediterranean nations, whole grains are commonly consumed with each meal.

At the next level of the Mediterranean food guide pyramid are fruits, vegetables, beans, other legumes, and nuts. A typical meal nearly always includes a salad that consists of dark green leafy lettuce, fresh vine-ripened tomatoes, broccoli, spinach, peppers, onions, and cucumbers. Fresh vegetables are often served, generally mixed with pasta or rice, used in salads, served as appetizers, or offered as a main dish or side dish. Fruit is eaten mainly as a dessert or as a snack.

Legumes and beans are generally served in soups or added to salads, used as dips (such as hummus), and are even offered as a main course. Nuts are often added to salads or to main dishes to add flavor and texture. Nuts are not usually consumed by themselves as they are in America—they are not a common appetizer served with high-sugar-content cocktails!

The third level up on the Mediterranean food guide pyramid is olive oil. This is used in place of margarine, butter, shortening, and other oils. Olive oil is not only used in cooking main dishes and side dishes, but it is routinely combined with balsamic vinegar to make a salad dressing.

The fourth level up on the Mediterranean food guide pyramid is cheese and yogurt. The diet uses very small amounts of cheese, such as freshly grated parmesan cheese on pasta, or a few crumbles of feta cheese on a Greek salad. Milk is usually not consumed as a beverage—rather, it is most commonly eaten in the form of yogurt (about a cup a day). Mediterranean Diet yogurt is not high in sugar, but is low fat or nonfat, served plain with fresh fruit added. A common use of yogurt is as a salad dressing—generally, with dill, garlic, onion, or cucumbers added to it.

Fish is the fifth level of the Mediterranean food guide pyramid. Fish is consumed far more frequently than red meat or poultry. In some Mediterranean nations, people eat up to thirty-eight ounces of fish per person per week.[2] Eating four-ounce portions of fish several times a week is very beneficial.

Poultry and eggs are at the sixth level up on the Mediterranean food guide pyramid. The typical Mediterranean diet includes three ounces of chicken two to four times a week. Fried chicken is virtually unknown in Mediterranean nations. Much of the chicken and turkey meat is skinned before the meat is cooked and added to soups, stews, and other vegetable-loaded dishes. Average egg consumption in these nations is from zero to four eggs a week. Generally, eggs are used in the making of breads and desserts—they are not a staple breakfast item.

At the seventh level of the pyramid are sweets. Typically, sweets, high-sugar desserts, and candies are not eaten daily. Rather, these are "treats" for birthdays, weddings, and other times of celebration. Dessert tends to be fresh fruit.

The top of the Mediterranean food guide pyramid is devoted to red meat. This includes the meat from beef, veal, pork, sheep, lamb, and goats. Red meat is rarely consumed more than a few times a month in Mediterranean nations, and is generally an "ingredient" mixed with small amounts of gravy and large amounts of vegetables, pasta, and rice. This meat tends to be reserved for special occasions and is rarely offered as a main course. Much of the meat is stewed or baked.

The Mediterranean Diet meals are usually served with red wine or bottled water as a beverage. Rarely is more than one glass consumed at a meal.

MORE THAN AN EATING PLAN

The Mediterranean Diet is more than an eating plan—it deals as well with the expenditure of calories and the social aspects of dining.

Exercise is common to the Mediterranean way of life. People who live in these nations usually do not exercise at health clubs or play sports; they are simply more active in the course of their everyday lives. They tend to walk to the market daily to buy fresh bread and produce, walk to their neighbors' homes to visit, and walk to work or school.

Those who live in Mediterranean nations also tend to eat in a more relaxed family-atmosphere setting. They enjoy sharing stories over meals, and they tend to take longer to consume meals, which are often interspersed with laughter. They savor their food and make dining an "experience," more than a chore.

The average American tends to spend no more than ten minutes at a meal, often staring at a television or driving in a car while eating. It's no wonder Americans suffer from a near epidemic of indigestion, heartburn, ulcer disease, gastritis, irritable bowel syndrome, and other digestive problems. In eating so quickly, Americans tend to shovel in a much larger amount of food than they really need; it takes a while for the brain to register the "full" signal, and by that time, most Americans have already overeaten.

Optimum digestion occurs when each bite of food is chewed approximately thirty times. This not only adds adequate saliva to the food, but sets the stage for optimal digestion and absorption. Plus, the slower pace of eating allows for the brain to send a more accurate signal that no more food is necessary.

Americans also tend to eat alone and to use food as a tranquilizer to relieve stress, anxiety, and depression. Mediterranean meals tend to be consumed with others present, and mealtime thus becomes a time for communication and emotional bonding. These attributes of dining help relieve stress and depression.

MAKING THE CHANGE TO A MEDITERRANEAN HEALTHSTYLE

These are the ten major steps I recommend for a person to change from a typical American way of eating to a Mediterranean way of eating:

1. Eliminate all processed foods from your cupboards, and start over. Toss all potato chips, corn chips, and other snack foods with hydrogenated fat, cookies, cakes, candies, crackers, high-sugar cereals, white bread, highly processed foods, and high-sugar foods. Also toss all oils other than olive oil, including any salad dressings, lard, Crisco, and other products that have hydrogenated fat. Begin to buy only whole-grain food items and fresh fruits and vegetables. Stock your shelves with olive oil, nuts, seeds, and whole grains.

2. Cook and bake with whole-grain products. Eat more fresh fruits and vegetables, beans, legumes, and nuts.

3. Substitute olive oil for butter, margarine, salad dressings, and other oils. Avoid all fried or deep-fried foods.

4. Limit cheese intake to small amounts of parmesan or feta cheese (used on main dishes or salads). Do not eat blocks of cheese.

5. Eat lowfat, plain yogurt, add fruit, and sweeten it with Stevia (a natural substitute for sugar that has no harmful side effects).

6. Choose fish and poultry over red meat, and eat meat sparingly.

7. Cut out sugary sweets.

8. Enjoy a glass of red wine with lunch or dinner.

9. Exercise regularly—walk more.

10. Make dining an experience that you enjoy with others. Slow down your eating, savor your food, and enjoy sharing life with family and friends.

SETTING UP THE IDEAL PANTRY

The ideal pantry for eating the way Jesus ate would include these general food items:

Bread. Select whole-grain breads or whole-grain pita bread. If you are allergic to wheat, choose millet bread or brown rice bread (available at most health food stores).

Cereal. Choose GoLean soy cereal, All Bran, Fiber One, Shredded Wheat, Grape Nuts, Natural Granola (without any added sugar), old-fashioned oatmeal (not instant), or Oat Bran. If you are allergic to wheat, try millet cereal or any gluten-free whole-grain cereal.

Cheese. Choose parmesan (freshly grated or in a block you can grate yourself), part skim mozzarella, or feta cheese. If you are sensitive or allergic to dairy products, choose soy cheese. I recommend organic cheeses.

Eggs. Choose free-range eggs.

Fish. Choose fish with scales and fins. Avoid catfish and shellfish. Make sure that your fish is fresh and that it comes from unpolluted waters.

Fruit. Fresh is best. Frozen is acceptable. Avoid canned fruit packed in syrup.

Herbs and Spices. Many Mediterranean recipes call for garlic powder, parsley, Celtic salt (available at most health food stores), and black pepper.

Experiment with herbs and spices—they are a great way to add flavor to your cooking without adding fat or sugar.

Meat. Choose free-range meat. Avoid pork.

Milk. Choose skim milk and skim milk yogurt or cottage cheese. Soy milk, rice milk, and almond milk are good choices if a person is sensitive or allergic to dairy products.

Nuts. Almonds and walnuts are preferred nuts. Keep nuts sealed in bags after they are opened, and store them in your refrigerator or freezer.

Olive Oil. Choose extra virgin or virgin olive oil.

Pasta. Choose whole-grain pasta products. If you are allergic to wheat, try spelt or rice pasta.

Poultry. Choose chicken and turkey, preferably white-meat portions.

Soups and Broths. Choose low-sodium, low-fat natural soup broths (available at health food stores) that are low in food additives.

Starches. Other than pasta, choose brown rice or wild rice, beans, legumes, lentils, coarse cornmeal or polenta, and potatoes (fresh, never instant).

Sweets. Stock a little honey. Consider using Stevia (a natural food source that is very sweet and can be readily added to foods instead of artificial sweetener). It is good for diabetics and has no harmful side effects. You may also want to have a little naturally sweetened fruit spread (no sugar added).

Vegetables. Choose fresh or frozen. Low-sodium canned vegetables are acceptable on occasion. Choose especially these vegetables: asparagus, broccoli, cabbage, carrots, peppers, olives, onions, spinach, tomatoes, Brussels sprouts, cauliflower, collard greens, kale, squash, turnip greens, and zucchini. Choose dark green lettuce such as romaine lettuce over iceberg lettuce, which does not have nearly as many phytonutrients.

Vinegar. Choose balsamic, red wine, or apple cider.

Wine. Choose red.

Yogurt. Choose plain, skim, or low fat.

Remember always—what you bring home from the store is what you have available to eat. If you don't bring junk food home, you won't eat junk food at home!

CHAPTER THIRTEEN

A DAILY EATING PLAN AND A WEEK'S WORTH OF MENUS

THE FOUNDATION FOR EATING THE WAY JESUS ATE IS a set of principles for daily living. Certainly having three meals a day—breakfast, lunch, and dinner—can be a healthy way to live, as long as these meals are small and well balanced. Even smaller snacks in between meals can keep blood sugar levels balanced and provide maximum energy throughout the day.

ALWAYS EAT BREAKFAST

Breakfast is the most important meal of the day. Never skip breakfast! Breakfast literally means "breaking the fast." Breakfast usually comes ten to twelve hours after a person's last meal.

When it comes to breakfast, think of your metabolic rate as a fire in the fireplace. By morning, the fires of metabolism have all but gone out.

In order to get the fire going again, you need to eat a healthy breakfast.

Whole-grain bread is a good choice for breakfast, as are whole-grain cereal, plain unsweetened yogurt, and a piece of fruit.

MAKE LUNCH YOUR MAIN MEAL

In Mediterranean nations, lunch is the most elaborate meal of the day. Families often spend an hour or more around a table eating, and then take a short nap to wait out the heat of the day.

I recommend that you take your lunch with you to work and encourage your coworkers or friends who work nearby to do the same. Then, get together and enjoy eating your lunches. Don't waste the time it takes to drive to a restaurant, find a parking place, wait to be seated, only to wolf down your lunch because the lunch hour is almost over. Rather, get together with friends or coworkers, and have a picnic outside. Use your lunch hour as a time to talk and laugh in a relaxed atmosphere. Before or after eating, you may want to go for a walk with your friends, which will help keep the metabolic fires burning.

Always remember that the key to eating the way Jesus ate is to eat more natural foods and to eat in a relaxed atmosphere.

EAT AN EARLY, LIGHT DINNER

For the majority of Americans, the main meal of the day is dinner. I recommend that you eat as early in the evening as possible—this is especially important if you have a weight problem. After dinner, take a walk with your family or friends.

Dinner is a good time to have a large salad of dark green lettuce (such as romaine) and add other fresh vegetables as desired, such as carrots, onions, tomatoes, and cucumbers. The more brilliantly colored, the better!

Dinner is a good meal to eat in multiple courses. After a salad, you may want to have a small bowl of bean soup, lentil soup, broccoli soup (with parmesan cheese over it), or fresh vegetable soup. Have a piece of whole-grain bread, which you may want to dip in hummus or into a mix of extra virgin olive oil that has had a little ground pepper and balsamic vinegar added to it.

Limit your intake of fish or poultry to three to four ounces per serving. Rarely eat red meat. If you are eating vegetables as an entrée, have them steamed or lightly stir-fried, or eat them fresh. There's no rule that says a main dish needs to be cooked!

Choose a piece of fresh fruit for dessert.

Consider having one glass of red wine with your meal, or have four to eight ounces of filtered water to which you have added a squeeze of fresh lemon or lime juice. (You can also add a very small amount of Stevia to lemon or lime water to make lemonade or limeade.)

LIGHT SNACKS CAN BE EATEN

I recommend fruit for snacks, perhaps with a couple of ounces of unsweetened yogurt or low-fat cottage cheese.

KEEP SPECIAL FOODS
FOR SPECIAL OCCASIONS

Does this way of eating mean that you can never have a piece of birthday cake or a bowl of ice cream? No! Follow this simple rule: reserve special foods for special occasions. If you are trying to lose weight, of course, you will want to eliminate all high-sugar foods until you reach your weight goal.

DRINK PLENTY OF WATER

Be sure to drink at least two quarts of filtered or purified water a day. I recommend one to two eight-ounce glasses of water thirty minutes before a meal to aid digestion and to help prevent overeating, and then one to two glasses approximately two hours after a meal. Drinking excessive water during a meal slows down digestion.

TIPS FOR DINING OUT

The average American dines out several times a week. You'll probably find that the most nutritious and economic meals are the ones you can make at home. But if dining out is pleasurable and more convenient to you, here are several suggestions:

- Always ask for your salad to come undressed, and request olive oil and vinegar salad dressing served on the side.

- Split an entrée with another person. The serving size of meat, fish, or poultry is generally sufficient for two people, especially in this day of bigger and bigger portions. Add healthy vegetable side dishes such as broccoli, asparagus, spinach, or a baked potato without anything added to it.

- Ask the chef not to add any butter to the vegetables while cooking them.

- Choose vegetable-based soups rather than cream-based soups.

- Request whole-grain bread.

- For dessert, choose fresh fruit if it is available.

A WEEK OF MENUS

The following is not a recipe guide, but an "eating" guide for a week's worth of meals.

DAY 1

Breakfast

Four ounces of fresh-squeezed fruit juice or a small piece of fruit.

One portion of old-fashioned oatmeal, to which you have added walnuts or sliced almonds. You may also want to add berries or your choice of fruit to the cereal. I recommend blueberries, blackberries, raspberries, or strawberries.

Lunch

Tuna salad, consisting of two to three ounces of water-packed tuna, to which you have added chopped onions, chopped celery, tomatoes, cucumbers, and any other desired vegetable. Put the tuna salad on top of a bed of dark green lettuce (such as romaine). Use a balsamic vinegar and olive oil dressing. (See recipe on pg 214.)

Drink filtered or bottled water with a squeeze of lemon or lime. (Stevia optional.)

VINEGAR AND OLIVE OIL SALAD DRESSING

This is my favorite recipe for a vinegar-and-oil salad dressing:

6 tablespoons extra virgin olive oil

4 tablespoons balsamic vinegar

2 tablespoons freshly squeezed lemon juice

½ teaspoon Celtic salt (more as needed)

1 to 2 cloves of garlic (crushed)

Combine all of the ingredients—you may want to blend them in a food processor or blender. Store in a sealed container, and refrigerate.

Dinner

A salad of dark green vegetables, plus carrots, tomatoes, cucumbers. Use a balsamic vinegar and olive oil dressing.

A cup of lentil soup.

One piece of whole-grain bread or whole-grain pita bread dipped in hummus. (See recipe below.)

Four ounces of grilled salmon with steamed broccoli, sprinkled with parmesan cheese and served over one small serving of brown or wild rice.

One four-ounce glass of red wine or filtered water.

HUMMUS

Soak chickpeas or garbanzo beans overnight. Drain them well. For every two cups of chickpeas, add one quart of fresh water, and bring the chickpeas to a boil, then allow them to continue simmering for one to two hours (until tender).

Drain off the water, and place the chickpeas into a blender or food processor. Puree. Then for every two cups of chickpeas, add:

½ cup of tahini or less (depending on taste)
2 tablespoons of extra virgin olive oil
1 clove of garlic (finely minced)
juice from 2 medium-sized lemons (freshly squeezed)
½ to 1 teaspoon of Celtic salt
½ teaspoon ground cumin

Thoroughly blend until smooth. Adjust seasoning as desired. Place in an airtight container, and refrigerate. The mixture should last approximately five days.[1]

DAY 2

Breakfast
Four ounces of fresh-squeezed fruit juice or a small piece of fruit.

Whole-grain cereal or high-fiber cereal (such as GoLean soy cereal, All Bran, Fiber One, shredded wheat, or Grape Nuts).

Use skim milk, soy milk, rice milk, or almond milk on your cereal.

Lunch
Large dark green salad with other vegetables added. Add two ounces of turkey breast (sliced). Dress with a sprinkling of feta cheese and a dressing made with balsamic vinegar and olive oil.

One slice of whole-grain bread (dipped in hummus or extra virgin olive oil).

Filtered or bottled water with freshly squeezed lemon or lime juice. (Stevia optional.)

Dinner

Salad of dark green lettuce with vinegar and oil dressing.

Whole-grain pasta with marinara sauce, sprinkled with parmesan cheese. (See recipe.)

One four-ounce glass of red wine or filtered water.

MARINARA SAUCE

Add to one can of low-salt tomato sauce:

> 2-3 fresh tomatoes, chopped
> 2-3 garlic cloves (minced)
> 1 cup chopped onions
> 3 tablespoons extra virgin olive oil
> 1 teaspoon oregano
> 2 tablespoons chopped fresh parsley
> 2 teaspoons dried basil
> Celtic salt and pepper to taste

This sauce does not need to be cooked!

DAY 3

Breakfast

Four ounces of freshly squeezed fruit juice or one small piece of fruit.

Egg omelet with one whole egg (free-range) and two additional egg whites (egg substitute). Add sliced onions, tomatoes, mushrooms, peppers, and any other vegetable desired. Cook the omelet in a small amount of olive oil, and sprinkle it with parmesan or mozzarella cheese.

One slice of whole-grain toast with olive oil butter.

Lunch

Salad with balsamic vinegar and olive oil dressing.

A sandwich consisting of two slices of whole-grain bread and three to four ounces of chicken breast. Add slices of tomato and leaves of lettuce. I recommend you marinate the chicken breast overnight in extra virgin olive oil and red wine or cooking wine, and then grill it at lunchtime (or in the morning before packing your lunch for work).

Bottled or filtered water with freshly squeezed lemon or lime juice (Stevia optional).

Dinner

Salad with balsamic vinegar and olive oil dressing.

Small serving of broccoli soup.

Baked sea bass (three to four ounces) sprinkled with parmesan cheese.

Whole-grain bread (dipped in hummus).

Vegetables of your choice—steamed or stir-fried in olive oil, and sprinkled with parmesan cheese.

One four-ounce glass of red wine or filtered water.

DAY 4

Breakfast

Four ounces of freshly squeezed juice or a small piece of fruit.

Add a cup of berries (blueberries, raspberries, or strawberries) or melon (watermelon, honeydew, or cantaloupe) or pineapple or any other favorite fruit to four to six ounces of plain low-fat or no-fat yogurt.

One slice of whole-grain toast with olive oil butter.

Lunch

Brown or wild rice and beans (red beans, black beans, lima beans, or the bean of your choice).

Dark green salad with vegetables, dressed with vinegar and olive oil dressing.

Bottled or filtered water with freshly squeezed lemon or lime juice.

Dinner

Thin-crust, whole-grain pizza dressed with vegetables such as tomatoes, onions, mushrooms, and peppers. Use olive oil in place of any other oil in preparation of crust. Sprinkle with a small amount of part-skim-milk mozzarella cheese. (If eating out, have pizza maker go easy on the cheese, and request a thin-crust pizza.)

One four-ounce glass of red wine or filtered water.

DAY 5

Breakfast

Four ounces of freshly squeezed fruit juice or small piece of fruit.

One bowl of oat-bran hot cereal with walnuts or sliced almonds and berries of your choice. (Use Stevia as sweetener.) Add soy or skim milk if needed.

Lunch

Greek salad (salad greens with sliced cucumbers, Greek olives, crumbled feta cheese, chopped tomatoes, thinly sliced onions, thinly sliced bell pepper) dressed with balsamic vinegar and olive oil dressing.

One slice of whole-grain bread or whole-grain pita bread (served with hummus).

Filtered or bottled water with freshly squeezed lemon or lime juice and Stevia to taste.

Dinner

Green salad.

Grouper or Mahi-Mahi, grilled and served with brown or wild rice and steamed mixed vegetables.

Whole-grain bread (dipped in olive oil or hummus).

One four-ounce glass of red wine or filtered water.

DAY 6

Breakfast

Four ounces of freshly squeezed fruit juice or a small piece of fruit.

One slice of whole-grain toast topped with soy sausage.

One grapefruit.

Lunch

Chicken and brown rice soup (made with low-sodium chicken broth, chopped onions, one teaspoon of extra virgin olive oil, chopped celery, chopped parsley, Celtic salt, and pepper to taste).

Whole-grain pita bread.

Bottled or filtered water with freshly squeezed lemon or lime juice and Stevia to taste.

Dinner

Green salad.

Kabob with free-range extra lean beef fillet cube(s) and mushrooms, onions, tomatoes, and any other vegetable desired. Use no more than three to four ounces of beef. Or one free-range beef fillet (three to four ounces) with grilled or steamed vegetables on the side. (I suggest steamed broccoli sprinkled with parmesan if fillet option is chosen.)

Whole-grain dinner roll.

One four-ounce glass of red wine or filtered water.

DAY 7

Breakfast

Four ounces of freshly squeezed fruit juice or a small piece of fruit.

High-fiber cereal or natural granola (without any added sugar).

Add berries or desired fruit.

Lunch

Whole-grain pasta salad (made with whole-grain pasta, olive oil, chopped vegetables such as tomatoes, peppers, carrots, and chopped greens).

Bottled or filtered water with freshly squeezed lemon or lime juice and Stevia to taste.

Dinner

Green salad.

Chicken and rice casserole, or chicken and whole-grain rice (or other grain) with steamed vegetables.

One four-ounce glass of red wine or filtered water.

NOTES

Introduction

1. Gunther B. Paulien, Ph.D., *The Divine Philosophy and Science of Health and Healing* (Brushton, N.Y.: Teach Services, Inc., 1995), 202.
2. Eric Schlosser, *Fast Food Nation* (New York: Houghton Mifflin Co., 2001), 6.
3. Elizabeth Gleick, "Land of the Fat," *Time International Edition*, 25 Oct. 1999, 242.

Chapter 1

1. Andrew Barry, "Take a Whiff: Why International Flavors and Fragrances Look Tempting Right Now," *Barrons*, 20 July 1998.
2. Patrick Quillin, *Beating Cancer with Nutrition* (Tulsa, Oka.: Nutrition Times Press Inc.) 1998.
3. Gleick, "Land of the Fat."
4. According to the Japanese Education Ministry.
5. Robert A. Ronzio, *The Encyclopedia of Nutrition and Good Health*

(New York: Facts on File, Inc., 1997), 34.

6. Joseph M. Merdcola, D.O., The Potential Dangers of Sucralose, http://www.mercola.com/2000/dec/3/sucralose_dangers.htm

7. Michael Murray and Joseph Pizzorno, *Encyclopedia of Natural Medicine* (Rocklin, Calif.: Prima Health, 1998).

Chapter 2

1. Joan Nathan, *The Foods of Israel Today* (New York: Random House, 2001).

2. For more on this, see William Coleman, *Today's Handbook of Bible Times and Customs* (Minneapolis, Minn., 1984).

3. Globe Communications Corporation, *Healing Foods from the Bible* (Boca Raton, Fla.: American Media Mini Mags, Inc., 2001), 85.

4. Nathan, *The Foods of Israel Today*.

5. Rex Russell, *What the Bible Says About Healthy Living* (Ventura, Calif.: Regal Books, 1996).

6. Udo Erasmus, *Fats That Heal, Fats That Kill* (Burnaby, British Columbia, Canada: Alive Books, 1994).

7. Mitchell L. Gaynor et al., *Dr. Gaynor's Cancer Prevention Program* (New York: Kensington Publishing, 1999).

Chapter 3

1. Rabbi Yacov Lipschutz, *Kashruth* (Brooklyn, N.Y.: Mesorah Publications, 1988).

2. Ronzio, *The Encyclopedia of Nutrition and Good Health*.

3. J. Dyerberg et al., "Fatty Acid Composition of Plasma Lipids in Greenland Eskimos," *American Journal of Clinical Nutrition*, 28 (1975), 958–966.

4. Erasmus, *Fats That Heal, Fats That Kill*.

5. Don Colbert, *Walking in Divine Health* (Lake Mary, Fla.: Creation House, 1999).

Chapter 4

1. See "Mad Cow Disease in the U.S.," CBS News, 26 March 2001.
2. Erik Schlosser, *Fast Food Nation* (New York: Houghton Mifflin Co., 2001).
3. *Washington Post*, 13 April 2001.
4. Lipschutz, *Kashruth*.
5. See www.msnbc.com/news
6. Lipschutz, *Kashruth*.
7. Marc Linder, "I Gave My Employer a Chicken That Had No Bone: Joint Firm-State Responsibility for Line-Speed, Related Occupational Injuries," *Case Western Reserve Law Review*, 46: 1 (Fall 1995).
8. Frank B. Hu et al., "A Prospective Study of Egg Consumption and Risk of Cardiovascular Disease in Men and Women," *Journal of the American Medical Association*, 15 (1999), 1387–1395.

Chapter 5

1. Fred Wight, Manners and Customs of Bible Lands (Chicago: Moody Press, 1980).
2. Gaynor, *Dr. Gaynor's Cancer Prevention Program*.

Chapter 6

1. S. Linger et al., The Natural Pharmacy (Rockland, Calif.: Prima Publishing, 1999).
2. J. J. Michnovicz et al., "Induction of Estradiol Metabolism by Dietary Indole-3-Carbinol in Humans," *Journal of the National Cancer Institute*, 82 (1990), 947–949.
3. D. P. Burkitt, et al. "Dietary Fiber and Disease," A *Journal of the American Medical Association*, 229 (1974), 1068–1074.

Chapter 7

1. Ronzio, *The Encyclopedia of Nutrition and Good Health*.

2. Nancy Jenkins, *The Mediterranean Cookbook* (New York: Bantam Books, 1994).
3. Erasmus, *Fats That Heal, Fats That Kill*.
4. Nathan, *The Foods of Israel Today*.
5. D. Steinberg, "Antioxidants and the Prevention of Human Atherosclerosis," *Circulation*, 85 (1996), 2338–2344.
6. Ancel Keys et al. "The Diet and 15 Year Death Rate in the Seven Countries Study," *American Journal of Epidemiology*, 124: 6 (1986), 903–915.
7. Paulien, *Divine Philosophy and Science of Health and Healing*.
8. James and Phyllis Balch, *Prescription for Nutritional Healing* (New York: Avery, 2000).
9. Allen Swenson, *Plants of the Bible* (New York: Carol Publishing, 1994).

Chapter 8

1. Earl D. Radmacker et al., *Nelson's New Illustrated Bible Commentary* (Nashville: Thomas Nelson, 1999), 1369.
2. David Whitten et al., *To Your Health* (New York: Harper-Collins Publishers, 1994).
3. S. Renaud and M. de Lorgeril, "Wine, Alcohol, Platelets and the French Paradox for Coronary Heart Disease," *Lancet*, 339 (1992), 1523–1526.
4. J. M. Gaziano et al., "Moderate Alcohol Intake, Increased Levels of High-Density Lipoprotein and Its Subfractions, and Decreased Risk of Myocardial Infarction," *New England Journal of Medicine*, 329 (1993), 1829–1843.
5. A. Klatsky et al., "Alcohol and Mortality: A Ten Year Kaiser-Permanente Experience," *Annals of Internal Medicine*, 95:2 (1981), 139–145.
6. Mark Hlatkymdetal, "Clinical Correlates of the Initial and Long-Term Cost of Coronary Bypass Surgery and Coronary Angioplasty," *American Heart Journal*, 138:2 (1999), 376–383.

7. Harlan Krumholz et al., "Clinical Correlates of In-Hospital Costs for Acute Myocardial Infarction in Patients 65 years of Age and Older," *American Heart Journal*, 135:3 (1998), 523–531.

8. M. Weisse et al., "Wine as a Digestive Aid: Comparative Antimicrobial Effects of Bismuth Salicylate in Red and White Wine," *British Medical Journal*, 311 (1995), 1457–1460.

9. G. Curhan et al., "Prospective Study of Beverage Use and a Risk of Kidney Stones," *American Journal of Epidemiology*, 143:5 (1996), 487–494.

10. E. B. Rimm et al., "Review of Moderate Alcohol Consumption and Reduced Risk of Coronary Heart Disease: Is the Effect Due to Beer, Wine, or Spirits?" *British Medical Journal*, 312 (1996), 731–736.

11. Cynthia Kuhn et al., Buzzed: The Straight Facts About the Most Used and Abused Drugs from Alcohol to Ecstasy (New York: W. W. Norton & Company, 2003), 57. See also the web site for The National Institute on Alcohol Abuse and Alcoholism (NIAAA) http://www.niaaa.nih.gov/ and the article "Health Risks and Benefits of Alcohol Consumption" Vol. 24 No.1, 2000.

12. The National Institute on Alcohol Abuse and Alcoholism (NIAAA) http://www.niaaa.nih.gov/.

13. Whitten et al., To Your Health.

14. J. M. McGinnis et al., "Actual Causes of Death in the United States," *Journal of the American Medical Association*, 270 (1993), 2207–2212.

15. Whitten et al., To Your Health.

16. The CAGE test is from the Department of Pharmacology at the University of Colorado Health Science Center: http://www2.uchsc.edu/pharm/arc_misc/cage.asp.

17. S. E. Hyman et al., "Alcoholism," in *Scientific American Textbook of Medicine*, Ed. E. Rubenstein and D. Federman (New York: Scientific American, Inc., 1997), 1–14.

Chapter 9

1. Fred Wight, *Manners and Customs of Bible Lands*.
2. Balch, *Prescription for Nutritional Healing*.
3. Linger, *The Natural Pharmacy* (Rockland, Calif.: Prima Publishing, 1999).
4. Gaynor, *Gaynor's Cancer Prevention Program*
5. James Duke, *Herbs of the Bible* (Loveland, Colo.: Interweave Press, 1999).
6. Ibid.
7. Swenson, *Plants*.
8. D. C. Jarvis, *Folk Medicine*, 1958.

Chapter 10

1. Arthur Blessitt, "How Far Did Jesus and Mary Walk?" www.blessitt.com
2. M. Mogadam, *Every Heart Attack Is Preventable* (Washington: Lifeline Press, 2001).
3. S. Blair et al., "Physical Fitness and All-Cause Mortality: A Prospective Study of Healthy Men and Women," *Journal of the American Medical Association*, 262 (1989), 2395–2401.
4. Susan. Puhl et al., *ACSM Fitness Book* (Champaign, Ill.: Human Kinetic, 1998).
5. K. Cooper, *Regaining the Power of Youth* (Nashville: Thomas Nelson, Inc., 1998).
6. Ibid.
7. K. Cooper, *Antioxidant Revolution*.
8. P. D. Thompson, "Cardiovascular Complications of Visorous Physical Activity," *Arch Intern Med*, 156 (1996), 2297–2302.
9. Blair, "Physical Fitness."

Chapter 11

1. NIH Technology Assessment Conference Panel, "NIH Panel Estimated Their Failure," *Annals of Internal Medicine*, 119 (1993), 764–770.
2. Broda Barnes et al., *Hypothyroidism: The Unsuspected Illness* (New York: Thomas Crowell, 1976).

3. J. Braly, *Dr. Braly's Food Allergy and Nutrition Revolution* (New Canaan, Conn.: Keats, 1992).

Chapter 12
1. Keys et al., "The Diet and 15-Year Death Rate in the Seven Countries Study."
2. Jenkins, *The Mediterranean Cookbook*.

Chapter 13
1. Martha Shulman, *Mediterranean Light* (New York: Harper-Collins, 1989).

Thomas Nelson Publishers and Dr. Don Colbert thank
Ken and Debbie Gass, whose encouragement and enthusiasm
have been so instrumental in bringing this book from start to
completion. You and your family have lived the healthstyle
in this book and are a testament to its success.

BIBLIOGRAPHY

Balch, James. *Prescription for Nutritional Healing*. New York: Avery, 2000.

Barilla, Jean. *The Nutrition Super Book*, Volume 2: *The Good Fats and Oils*. New Canaan, Conn.: Keats Publishing, 1996.

Barnes, Broda, et al. *Hypothyroidism: The Unsuspected Illness*. New York: Thomas Crowell, 1976.

Blair, S., et al. "Physical Fitness and All-Cause Mortality: A Prospective Study of Healthy Men and Women." *Journal of the American Medical Association*, 262 (1989), 2395–2401.

Blessitt, Arthur. "How Far Did Jesus and Mary Walk?" www.blessitt.com

Burkitt, D.P. et al., "Dietary Fiber and Disease," *A Journal of the American Medical Association*, 229 (1974), 1068–1074.

Braly, J. *Dr. Braly's Food Allergy and Nutrition Revolution*. New Canaan, Conn.: Keats, n.d.

Colbert, Don, *Walking in Divine Health*. Lake Mary, Fla.: Creation House, 1999.

Coleman. *Today's Handbook of Bible Times and Customs*.

Cooper, Kenneth. *Antioxidant Revolution*. Nashville: Thomas Nelson, Inc., 1994.

———. *Regaining the Power of Youth*. Nashville: Thomas Nelson, Inc., 1998.

Curhan, G., et al. "Prospective Study of Beverage Use and a Risk of Kidney Stones." *American Journal of Epidemiology*, 143:5 (1996), 487–494.

Duke, James. *Herbs of the Bible*. Loveland, CO: Interweave Press, 1999.

Dyerberg, J., et al. "Fatty Acid Consumption of Plasma Lipids in Greenland Eskimos." *American Journal of Clinical Nutrition*, 28 (1975), 958–966.

Erasmus, Udo. *Fats That Heal, Fats That Kill*. Burnaby, British Columbia, Canada: Alive Books, 1994.

Gaynor, Mitchell L., et al. *Dr. Gaynor's Cancer Prevention Program*. New York: Kensington Publishing, 1999.

Gaziano, J. M., et al. "Moderate Alcohol Intake, Increased Levels of High-Density Lipoprotein and Its Subfractions, and Decreased Risk of Myocardial Infarction." *New England Journal of Medicine*, 329 (1993), 1829–1843.

Globe Communications Corporation. *Healing Foods from the Bible*.

Hu, Frank B., et al. "A Prospective Study of Egg Consumption and Risk of Cardiovascular Disease in Men and Women." *Journal of the American Medical Association*, 281:15 (1999), 1387–1395.

Hyman, S. E., et al. "Alcoholism." In *Scientific American Textbook of Medicine*. Eds. E. Rubenstein and D. Federman. New York: Scientific American, Inc., 1997.

Jarvis, D. C. *Folk Medicine*. 1958.

Jenkins, Nancy. *The Mediterranean Cookbook*. New York: Bantam Books, 1994.

Keys, Ancel, et al. "The Diet and 15-Year Death Rate in the Seven Countries Study." *American Journal of Epidemiology*, 124 (1986), 903–1015.

Klatsky, A., et al. "Alcohol and Mortality: A Ten Year Kaiser-Permanente Experience." *Annals of Internal Medicine*, 95:2 (1981), 139–145.

Linger, S., et al. *The Natural Pharmacy*. Rockland, Calif.: Prima Publishing, 1999.

Lipschutz, Rabbi Yacov. *Kashruth*. Brooklyn, N.Y.: Mesorah Publications, 1988.

"Mad Cow Disease in the U.S." CBS News. March 26, 2001.

McGinnis, J. M., et al. "Actual Causes of Death in the United States." *Journal of the American Medical Association*, 270 (1993), 2207–2212.

Mogadam, M. *Every Heart Attack Is Preventable*. Washington: Lifeline Press, 2001.

Murray, Michael, and Joseph Pizzorno. *Encyclopedia of Natural Medicine*.

Nathan, Joan. *The Foods of Israel Today*. New York: Random House, 2001.

NIH Technology Assessment Conference Panel. "NIH Panel Estimated Their Failure." *Annals of Internal Medicine*, 119 (1993), 764–770.

Paulien, Gunther B., Ph.D. *The Divine Philosophy and Science of Health and Healing*. Brushton, N.Y.: Teach Services, Inc., 1995.

Potential Dangers of Sucralose, The. http://www.mercola.com/2000/dec/3/sucralose_dangers.htm

Puhl, S., et al. *ACSN Fitness Book*. Champaign, Ill.: Human Kinetic, 1998.

Quillin, Patrick. *Beating Cancer with Nutrition*. Tulsa, Okla.: Nutrition Times Press Inc., 1998.

Renaud, S., and M. de Lorgeril. "Wine, Alcohol, Platelets and the French Paradox for Coronary Heart Disease." *Lancet*, 339 (1992), 1523–1526.

Rimm, E. B., et al. "Review of Moderate Alcohol Consumption and Reduced Risk of Coronary Heart Disease: Is the Effect Due to Beer, Wine, or Spirits?" *British Medical Journal*, 312 (1996), 731–736.

Ronzio, Robert A. *The Encyclopedia of Nutrition and Good Health*. New York: Facts on File, Inc., 1997.

Russell, Rex. *What the Bible Says About Healthy Living.* Ventura, Calif.: Regal Books, 1996.

Schlosser, Eric. *Fast Food Nation.* New York: Houghton Mifflin Co., 2001.

Shulman, Martha. *Mediterranean Light.* New York: Harper-Collins, 1989.

Steinberg, D. "Antioxidants and the Prevention of Human Atherosclerosis." *Circulation* 85 (1996), 2338–2344.

Swenson, Allan. *Plants of the Bible.* New York: Carol Publishing Group, 1994.

Walker, G. B., D. P. Burkitt, et al. "Dietary Fiber and Disease." *Journal of the American Medical Association,* 229 (1973), 1068–1074.

Washington Post, April 13, 2001.

Weisse, M., et al. "Wine Is a Digestive Aid: Comparative Antimicrobial Effects of Bismuth Salicylate in Red and White Wine." *British Medical Journal,* 311 (1995), 1457–1460.

Wight, Fred. *Manners and Customs of Bible Lands.* Chicago, Ill.: Moody Press, 1980.

Whitten, David, et al. *To Your Health.* New York: Harper-Collins Publishers, 1994.

ABOUT THE AUTHOR

Don Colbert, M.D., BOARD CERTIFIED IN FAMILY practice since 1987, is the author of such bestsellers as *Toxic Relief, Deadly Emotions, Walking in Divine Health, What You Don't Know May Be Killing You*, and The Bible Cure Booklet Series. He writes monthly columns for *Charisma* magazine and Joyce Meyers's *Partners* magazine. Dr. Colbert has been featured in *News Week, Reader's Digest, L.A. Times, Esquire* magazine, and has also been a guest on news programs such as National Fox Live, CBS News, and CBN News. He developed his own vitamin line, Divine Health Nutritional Products, and hosts a national talk show entitled *Your Health Matters* with his wife, Mary. He regularly speaks at national seminars and conferences on such topics as "The Seven Pillars of Health," "Deadly Emotions," and other health related topics. He makes his home in the Orlando, Florida area.

YOU MAY CONTACT DR. COLBERT AT:

www.drcolbert.com

or

(407)331-7007

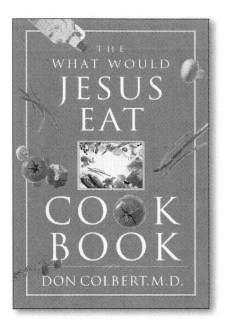

B ased on a biblical and historical study of what Jesus ate, as well as scientific research on why these particular foods are ideal for healthy living, *What Would Jesus Eat?* is the ultimate program for eating well in the twenty-first century.

Now, this companion cookbook helps readers to creatively and practically incorporate these foods into their own diets. These easy-to-follow recipes are designed to help the reader prepare foods commonly eaten during the time of Christ in a way that will satisfy modern-day palates. Dishes feature fresh fruits and vegetables, whole grains, legumes, fish, olive oil, and more. This unique cookbook is ideal for anyone desiring to safely lose weight or simply eat healthier.

ISBN 0-7852-6519-8

I f you haven't met my best friend, Jesus, I would like to take this oppor-tunity to introduce Him to you. It is very simple.

If you are ready to let Him come into your heart and become your best friend, just bow your head and sincerely pray this prayer from your heart:

Lord Jesus, I want to know You as my Savior and Lord. I believe You are the Son of God, and that You died for my sins. I also believe You were raised from the dead and now sit at the right hand of the Father praying for me. I ask You to forgive me for my sins and change my heart so that I can be Your child and live with You eternally. Thank You for Your peace. Help me to walk with You so that I can begin to know You as my best friend and my Lord.

Amen

If you have prayed this prayer, we rejoice with you in your decision and your new relationship with Jesus. Please contact a local church in your area and attend regularly. Begin reading the Bible daily, starting with the book of Matthew.